MAHARAJA
RAJENDRA NARAYAN SINGH DEO

Praise for the book

'This is a very worthwhile and readable book that brings to life an individual of exceptional qualities and noble character. Here, we have a public spirited and patriotic ruler. This is a well-written book and worth reading.'

—Maharaja Captain Amarinder Singh
Former Chief Minister of Punjab,
Head of the Royal House of Patiala State

'Hidden in the pages of history are gems of great lustre like R.N. Singh Deo, the former chief minister (CM) of Orissa, who strode like a colossus in the nascent politics of independent India. Although belonging to royalty, he was the quintessential democrat, an enlightened leader, an able administrator and a highly cultured human being. The history of modern India cannot be fully understood unless we read the lives and times of such outstanding men.'

—Pavan K. Varma
Author, Diplomat and
Former Member of Parliament, Rajya Sabha

'R.N. Singh Deo was not only Maharaja but an elected CM of Orissa during the most difficult time for non-Congress parties. I had met him in the early 1970s when we all came together for a conference called by Shri Morarji Desai and others. I was much impressed by his humility and knowledge, and that inspired me. He was a maharaja and a CM despite being in his early 30s.

He also set up many colleges for higher studies and teaching Sanskrit in Orissa. He was a prince among men and a man amongst princes. His family's lineage goes all the way back to the ancient Dakshina Kosala of Kusha, who was the second son of Lord Rama and Sita. Maharaja Singh Deo can be truly called the initiator of the consolidation of opposition parties, which ultimately led to the formation of the Janata Party and the overthrow of the Emergency foisted by Mrs Indira Gandhi. He will always remain immortal in the memories of the people of India and, in particular, Orissa for his magnificent contribution as the ruler of the erstwhile state of Patna, as CM of Orissa and a political statesman.

—Dr Subramanian Swamy
Former Member of Parliament,
Former Minister of Commerce and Industry and Law and Justice

'His Highness (HH) Maharaja Rajendra Narayan Singh Deo was an unusual prince. He was a public spirited, astute politician, who was fair-minded and cool-headed. He preferred humility to arrogance, simplicity to showmanship. At crucial moments in the history of post-1947 Orissa, he played the role of a far-sighted statesman. He was tactfully firm with his fellow princes of Orissa and Chhattisgarh, warning them that they must face reality or perish. The result was the smooth accession and end of arbitrary rule. Almost 20 years later, he again acted with wisdom. In 1967, at the meeting of the All India Congress Committee in Shimla, the late Chandra Shekhar tabled a resolution seeking the abolition of princely privileges and privy purses. Mrs Indira Gandhi was not present at the meeting. She played for time, but a rump of princes called the 'concord' forced her hand in 1970. I took the Maharaja to meet the prime minister (PM). He told her that he would go along with her decision. This was statesmanship. K.C. Pant was at the time minister of state in the home ministry. His meeting with Maharaja Singh Deo left a very favourable impression on the young minister, who was in charge of the question on privy purse and privileges. As CM of Orissa—more than once—as Member of Parliament (MP) and as founder of the All India Ganatantra Parishad, he functioned with efficient skill. His relations with the formidable Biju Patnaik were cordial, even though they were on opposite sides of the political fence. His services to Orissa, its people and his memory will endure.'

—K. Natwar Singh
Former Minister of External Affairs,
Member of the Royal House of Bharatpur State

'Through their thorough research and instructive narrative, the authors have shed light on a towering figure who had till recently been relegated to the footnotes of our history books. In fluent and engaging prose, they have offered an instructive study of a leader truly ahead of his time and a prince who became a democratic politician. A consummate synthesizer of tradition and progress, an understated reformer and prescient administrator, Maharaja Rajendra Narayan Singh Deo was not just an instrumental force behind the creation of the modern state of Odisha as we know it, but a tireless champion of the people he passionately spent his life caring for. Through his actions, he, in many ways, personified and animated the dream of a united democratic India and the aspirations of her people at the turn of their transition from the colonial era to that of contemporary freedom. While there is room to disagree with some of the references to the Congress party and its leaders in this volume, it offers stimulating material for learning and discussion. I am pleased to recommend it to a broad readership.'

—Dr Shashi Tharoor

Member of Parliament for Thiruvananthapuram,
Former Minister of State of External Affairs and Author

'The fall of empires after the Second World War led to the dawn of modern democratic nations. In order to ensure a safe transition from empire to nation, rulers of princely India, alongside political pioneers, set aside their interests and came together to create what we know as India today. My great-granduncle Nawab Hamidullah Khan and Shri R.N. Singh Deo stood together in that crucial time as close allies and are remembered today as statesmen well ahead of their time. As India raged through industrialization, economic development, the political ebb and flow in its post-Independence years, the fast pace of time as well as ever-changing milieus led to an overlooked past and forgotten heritage. The decisions, practices and ideology of the erstwhile rulers were not only revolutionary in their time, but are relevant even today.'

—Sahebzada Omar Faruq Ali

Educator and Member of the Royal House of Bhopal State

'He was a wise and benevolent ruler of his state, a statesman, a sincere politician, a successful CM and Union Cabinet Minister. But above all, he was a gentle and cultured human being. He particularly attracted my attention and admiration, not only because he was the first non-Congress CM but also because he hailed from an erstwhile princely state of Patna. He further appealed to my imagination as he had successfully achieved the dream of my father Maharaja Hanwant Singh—also the last ruling prince of the state of Jodhpur—for a smooth transition from a hereditary ruler to a democratically elected leader of his state. He went on to be a great reformist ruler of his state with many firsts to his credit, like opening up temples for the Dalits, starting with his own palace temple, abolishing child marriage and bringing about many other liberal reforms, like modernizing the administrative and legal institutions of the state, including a more equitable and just system of land revenue records. He brought the same experience and connect with people into his role as a successful CM and Cabinet Minister.'

—Maharaja Gaj Singh
Former Member of Parliament,
Head of the Royal House of Jodhpur State

'I have had the great honour of maintaining my family's generational friendship with the family of the late Maharaja Rajendra Narayan Singh Deo of Patna State. As time passed, I have come to know this great king through anecdotes and his legacy that his family proudly carries forward. This book greatly enriches an untold yet magnificent legacy of a visionary ruler and how he harnessed his abilities for the cause of a young and evolving nation.'

—Maharaja Sawai Padmanabh Singh
International Polo Player,
Head of the Royal House of Jaipur State

'Shri R.N. Singh Deo was a leader ahead of his time. He was noted for his unwavering determination to serve his people. His tenacity and altruistic beliefs were what gained him mighty popularity and endearment, not his royal title or position as heir to a state. Much of his work as a statesman can be called revolutionary for the many "firsts" he introduced in state administration, polity and judicial system.'

—Maharaja Jyotiraditya Madhavrao Scindia
Union Minister for Civil Aviation and Steel,
Head of the Royal House of Gwalior State

'There are people who are born to rule and there are rulers who are born to serve their subjects. Shri Rajendra Narayan Singh Deo belongs to the rare class of royalty that presents a classic blend of both. He was a kind-hearted king, an able administrator, a revolutionary reformist, a vigilant visionary and a simple soul. He ruled the hearts of the people of his province during the pre-Independence era and thereafter the entire state of Orissa as its dynamic CM. And this he did through his pioneering work in the field of education, health, social welfare, cooperative movement, land enactments, revenue and judicial reforms, etc. A true Gandhian, Shri Rajendra Narayan believed in simplicity, fairness, uprightness, transparency, moral values in public life and led by his own example. He instituted a rare inquiry to probe into charges of corruption against himself that were levelled by the Opposition. He was a man of high morals and profound integrity, which earned him respect from across the political spectrum.

—(Late) Maharaja Virbhadra Singh
Former Chief Minister of Himachal Pradesh,
Head of the Royal House of Bushahr State

'Rajendra Narayan Singh Deo has a unique place in Orissa's history. His rich contribution to the social, administrative, political and cultural life of Orissa has had a considerable bearing on the lives of all the people of Orissa to this day. He championed the cause of upliftment of the poor. He introduced social reforms, like allowing entry of the underprivileged in temples and shunned the social evil of child marriage. These point towards his humane, people-centric and democratic approach aimed at benefitting the people of Orissa.

He can be best described as a leader who was ahead of his time and who worked selflessly for the welfare and upliftment of all and believed that the rule of law [nyaya] and conduct [dharma] must go hand in hand.'

—Piyush Goyal
Minister of Commerce & Industry,
Consumer Affairs & Food & Public Distribution and Textiles and
Leader of House in Rajya Sabha

'This well-researched and well-written biography of Maharaja Rajendra Narayan Singh Deo of the Patna State of Balangir in Orissa is a valuable addition to the study of modern Indian history, which is marked by an insufficient appreciation of the contributions made by the princely rulers to the socio-economic development of modern India and their sacrifice of power and wealth for the betterment of independent India.

Maharaja Singh Deo was not just a progressive and reformist princely ruler but also a leader of the Indian national movement and the former CM of the state of Orissa. This book documents the known and lesser known facets of the life of the Maharaja and the historical processes that led to the integration of the princely states into the Indian Union.'

—Maharaja Samarjitsinh Gaekwad
Head of the Royal House of Baroda State

'Maharaja Singh Deo had a clear vision for his people; he remains an icon for Indian royalty and an enigma for the people of Balangir and Orissa. This body of work celebrating the life of a great reformer of India shines bright in the age of historical records being set straight for future generations.'

—Nawab Syed Muhammad Kazim Ali Khan
Former State Minister for Minority Welfare and Hajj Affairs,
Head of the Royal House of Rampur State

'A giant among men, his unique contribution to the social, political, economic and cultural fields of Odisha are unparalleled and will never be surpassed.'

—Dr Ramakanta Panda
Padma Vibhushan Awardee,
Heart Surgeon at Asian Heart Institute, Bombay

'The last ruling Maharaja of Patna was truly a man among princes. His venerable connection with his subjects and voters must be studied closely by those engaged in public life today.'

—Maharaja Ranjeet Singh Judeo
Head of the Royal House of Samthar State
Former Home Minister, Government of Uttar Pradesh

MAHARAJA
RAJENDRA NARAYAN SINGH DEO

A Man Among Princes

PABITRA MOHAN NAYAK | V.R. SINGH

RUPA

First published by
Rupa Publications India Pvt. Ltd 2022
7/16, Ansari Road, Daryaganj
New Delhi 110002

Sales Centres:

Allahabad Bengaluru Chennai
Hyderabad Jaipur Kathmandu
Kolkata Mumbai

Photo credit: Author Archive

ISBN: 978-93-5520-316-8

First impression 2022

10 9 8 7 6 5 4 3 2 1

Printed in India.

Contents

Foreword *xiii*

1. Destiny's Child 1
2. A Wise Ruler 17
3. The Merger 38
4. The Lost Districts 61
5. Palace to Parliament 83
6. Politics and Statecraft 98
7. Biju Patnaik's Intervention 108
8. Death of a Coalition 114
9. The Turbulent '60s 122
10. Chief Minister Singh Deo 132
11. A Play of Politics 139
12. Back to Balangir 157
13. Man and Statesman 161

Epilogue 168
Acknowledgements 171
Bibliography 174
Index 179

Foreword

The integration of almost 600 princely states into the Union was a historic achievement—probably the most peaceful transition from feudalism to democracy anywhere in the world. For this achievement, Sardar Patel, the then home minister and deputy PM certainly deserves full credit. However, one point is generally missed out: this was only possible due to the patriotic collaboration of the princes themselves, for which they have seldom received any credit. Even during the reign of the British, a great deal of economic development and political empowerment took place in many of the erstwhile princely states with the help of rulers who were positive and forward-looking. This understanding, of course, requires massive academic research, which is long overdue.

This book is about one such progressive prince, Maharaja Rajendra Narayan Singh Deo of Patna State in Orissa. Having ruled for many years prior to Independence, he had brought about remarkable reforms in the legislative, executive and judiciary. He was a scholar, a sportsman, a patron of art and culture and, surprisingly, an exponent of the world-famous Seraikela Chhau dance. He established several educational institutions, including a teacher's training school, an industrial school and Sanskrit Vidyalaya in Orissa. In the political field, he set up a legislative Assembly of 20 members, of which half were elected and half were nominated. He took a strong stand against untouchability and enacted laws to allow the Harijans[1] to enter the temples, similar to what my father Maharaja Hari Singh did in Jammu and Kashmir (J&K) in 1929.

After Independence, he was the first ruler to sign the instrument of merger with the Union. The state of Patna was merged with Orissa and now comprises the district of Balangir. With his alacrity of body and mind, it was inevitable that Maharaja Rajendra Narayan would join politics. He formed a regional political party called the Ganatantra Parishad (GP) from which he was elected to the first Lok Sabha in 1951. In 1957, he was elected to the Orissa Legislative Assembly, where he became leader of the opposition. Later, in 1962, the GP merged with the Swatantra Party. In March 1967, he was the first former Maharaja to become CM of Orissa which, by a strange coincidence, was exactly the time when I spearheaded the transition from feudalism to democracy by moving from J&K and enjoining Mrs Indira Gandhi's Cabinet.

It was during his period of chief ministership that the Maharaja invited me to address the convocation in Balangir over which he presided. I flew there with him in a small plane from Bhubaneswar and enjoyed visiting his hometown and interacting with the students. I enjoyed his company, as he was an interesting conversationalist, and I have good memories of my association with him. His services to his state and then to Orissa will be remembered for long.

---

[1]The term 'Harijan' was coined by Mahatma Gandhi as an attempt to change the way the Dalit community was perceived, proclaiming them to be children of God holding a right to worship.

I am glad that the two authors, Pabitra Mohan Nayak and Kunwar V.R. Singh, have produced this interesting biography of Maharaja Rajendra Narayan Singh Deo and I congratulate his son, Shri Ananga Uday Singh Deo, for bringing out this important account of history.

—Maharaja Dr Karan Singh
Former Union Minister for Tourism,
Civil Aviation, Health and Education,
Former Sadr-e-Riyasat of J&K
and Head of the Royal House of J&K State

1

Destiny's Child

It is said that any office is what the holder makes of it. This is true for both elected office as well as a royal darbaar. Statecraft in India has mostly remained a family affair. With time, democratic values have grown on a society that has for a large period of time remained inherently undemocratic. Indian royalty was largely censured in the history books, often described as polo-playing tyrannies, deranged nymphomaniacs obsessed with purebred dogs, horses and opiates. This unfair treatment has unfortunately not witnessed a credible rebuttal. Only in the past decade, Indian royalty has embraced a new image of being connoisseurs of exquisite cooking and wine. But far beyond the polo-playing, mutton recipes and fashion statements, there existed a glorious legacy of kings accompanied with genuine reform.

Many of the maharajas, after signing the Instrument of Accession, remained in active public service one way or another. Even their children never lost their sense of service to the people of their erstwhile kingdoms. Many shining examples can be looked at till this day. HH Capt. Amarinder Singh of Patiala is one of the tallest politicians in Punjab, not on account of his legacy, but purely on the merits of his performance as CM. Rajmata Vijayaraje Scindia of Gwalior played a key role in the formation and structure of the Jana Sangh and the Bharatiya Janata Party (BJP). In the western part of India, Maharaj Chandra Vir Singh Jaisalmer is remembered today as a man who represented the true voice of his people. Kunwar Natwar Singh of Bharatpur went on to became minister of external affairs and is also a Padma Bhushan awardee.

The great poet John Milton said, 'Yet he who reigns within himself, and rules Passions, Desires, and Fears, is more a King.' Royalty in India has displayed spectacular majesty and sacrifice for the cause of the new Indian republic, far more than it is given credit for in the records of history. To this day, the children and grandchildren of Maharaja Rajendra Narayan Singh Deo have been involved in the state politics after him. His grandchildren, Rajkumars Kalikesh Singh Deo and Arkesh Singh Deo, are politicians poised to lead the state in the future. Rajkumar Manmath Singh Deo, the second of the three grandsons of the Maharaja, managed three consecutive state Assembly elections as a masterful strategist before moving into business and is remembered as a powerful and popular political force in Balangir even today. The present maharaja of the erstwhile princely state of Patna, Kanak Vardhan Singh Deo, represented Balangir district as minister and headed the BJP in Orissa. His younger brother, Maharajkumar Srivardhan Singh Deo of Patna, has lent his keen sense of politics and statecraft in many electoral strategies and remains a steadfast pillar of support to the Patna royal family in political affairs.

ROYAL SACRIFICE FOR UNITY

Historians of modern India have celebrated the deliberations and efforts of both Sardar Vallabhbhai Patel[1] and secretary, V.P. Menon, towards the integration of India—undoubtedly an extraordinary achievement—but have largely overlooked the contribution of the Indian princes. They gave away their entire kingdoms to the idea of a new India, an India that would eventually become an economic force on the verge of being able to lead the world again, a little over three-quarters of a century later. PM Narendra Modi acknowledged this contribution of the Indian princes at a ceremony in Gujarat in 2019, becoming the only elected head of government to do so.[2]

Most of the Indian royalty and princely states, with the zamindaris[3], jagirs and thikanas[4] were under the suzerainty of the British as against provinces that were British territories and directly administered by the colonial government known as British India. Even the British tried to integrate the princely states during the Raj, but failed.[5] In fact, at the time of

---

[1]India's first deputy PM and home minister.

[2]WildFilmsIndia, 'PM Modi's Speech | Inauguration of Statue of Unity in Gujarat', Youtube, 29 August 2019, https://bit.ly/3JdBepG. Accessed on 4 March 2022.

[3]Under the zamindari system, zamindars or landowners held land. The East India Company under Lord Cornwallis, realizing this, introduced the Permanent Settlement of 1793 among the zamindars and made them proprietors of their land in return for a fixed annual rent.

[4]The estates of the Thakurs were called thikanas.

[5]The British made several attempts to integrate the princely states more closely with British India, by creating the Chamber of Princes as a consultative and advisory body in 1921, and creating direct relations in 1936 between the Government of India and the larger princely states, superseding political agents. The ambitious plan envisaged the princely states and British India being united under a federal government. This scheme was abandoned in 1939 following the outbreak of the Second World War.

the British withdrawal, 565 princely states were officially recognized in the Indian subcontinent, apart from thousands of zamindari estates and jagirs.[6] It was indeed both the idea of an independent nation considering the interests of its subjects as well as the paramountcy and might of a federal union of states, coupled with Patel's spectacular diplomacy and iron will that each monarch eventually made the decision to accede to India. No doubt, the subcontinent would have achieved even greater heights had the deeply flawed two-nation theory been nipped in the bud and not permitted to move beyond drawing-room discussions.

Piece by piece, by diplomacy or sword, each section of the political map we notice today was built as a result of the sacrifices of the states and the hard work put in by both Patel and Menon. The royals remained citizens with privilege, even when their titles were withdrawn by Indira Gandhi. And even today, they are respected by the subjects in their erstwhile estates and lands, being an important part of religious and customary congregation.

Most of the Indian royal houses followed the rule of primogeniture for succession. The society was largely patriarchal barring exceptions such as Travancore and Bhopal. In the case of no male heirs, the rulers would often adopt a male successor to be the ruler. This was common among childless Rajput kings. In fact, Maharaja Rajendra became the king as the result of an adoption.

He was originally born into the royal family of Seraikela—an Odia princely state now in modern-day Jharkhand—but adopted by Maharaja Prithviraj Singh Deo of Patna State, 450 km southwest of Seraikela with its capital in Balangir. Maharaja

---

[6]Bhargava, R.P., *The Chamber of Princes*, Northern Book Centre, 1991, pp. 312–23.

Rajendra Narayan Singh Deo was born on 31 March 1912 to the last ruler of Seraikela Raja Aditya Pratap Singh Deo and Rani Padmini Kumari Devi, daughter of Ramachandra Singh Deo of Patna state. Rani Padmini's intriguing story deserves further exploration, as years later she set aside her scarred history with the Patna lineage of her clan and allowed the adoption of her son into the very family from where she had narrowly escaped as a little girl. After the first war of independence in 1857, Patna existed as a princely state, subject to the suzerainty of the British Crown. In 1912, the British reconstituted the region and formed the Bihar and Orissa Province and the tributary states, also known as Garjats that were administratively controlled by the Orissa commissioner, who was headquartered at Cuttack. The Garjats play a vital role in the politics of the region even to this day.

While the rulers of the princely state of Patna hailed from the Chauhan dynasty, Seraikela belonged to the Rathore dynasty, established by its founder Raja Bikram Singh in 1620.[7]

POWER PLAYS FOR THE THRONE

The twenty-sixth Chauhan ruler of Patna, Maharaja Sura Pratap who reigned between 1866 and 1878 had no male heir. Consequently, he adopted his brother Biswanath's son, Ramchandra Singh Deo, who assumed the throne from 1878 to 1895. However, the third brother, Dalganjan Singh did not approve of this adoption considering himself to be the rightful heir to the throne. His often-malicious and failed attempts to instigate dissent against the throne annoyed the British, who banished him from the state. The order of banishment was, however, withdrawn on a representation of Maharaja

[7]'Saraikela', Britannica, https://bit.ly/35J5tXS. Accessed on 13 March 2022.

Ramchandra Singh Deo who wanted his thread ceremony to be performed by Dalganjan, his uncle. But Dalganjan did not reform his conniving ways. Eventually, Maharaja Ramchandra, who was married to the princess of Lanjigarh, became a victim to Dalganjan's conspiracy against the throne.

Dalganjan's influence on the Rani and his desperate quest for the throne resulted in tragedy, when an inflamed Maharaja Ramchandra gunned down his own Maharani and then himself. Maharaja Ramchandra's infant daughter Padmini Kumari was saved by a quick-thinking and brave maidservant, and brought up by the dowager Maharani of Sura Pratap. She grew up to be accomplished at art and dance, and was married at a young age to Raja Aditya Pratap Singh Deo of Seraikela. In the meantime, Dalganjan, as a result of his sinister conspiracy, succeeded to the throne as HH Dalganjan Singh Deo of Patna State in 1895.[8] However, unbeknownst to him, his own son HH Prithviraj Singh Deo would go on to adopt Padmini Kumari's son, as the future maharaja of Patna State!

DRAMA OF SUCCESSION

Maharaja Dalganjan Singh died in 1910 and his son Prithviraj succeeded him. He commissioned the construction of the Sailashree Palace in Balangir—a magnificent building that was finally completed by Maharaja Rajendra. The locals referred to it as Badal Mahal because of its soaring height with lofty towers and spires. The palace today remains an impressive example of non-Odia architecture. While Badal Mahal was still under construction, Prithviraj remained uncertain about

---

[8]Gopabandhu Academy of Administration, 'Appendix II: Events leading to Adoption of Rajendra Narayan Singh Deo', *Odisha District Gazetteers,* https://bit.ly/3KhRXcL. Accessed on 21 March 2022.

the future, as he had no children from any of his queens. His brother Batsraj Singh Deo had one son. However, his request to adopt Batsraj's son had been denied. Recovering from a prolonged illness, Prithviraj had grown even more anxious over his inability to find a successor.

Search for an Heir

In 1914, Prithviraj was on his way to Kolkata when he decided to break his journey for a day at Sini Junction railway station to proceed to Seraikela and visit his niece Padmini Kumari. He was fond of her, despite their tragic family history. Moreover, she went on to be a mother of nine children—three daughters and six sons—one of whom he adopted as his successor.

Upon his visit to Seraikela, Prithviraj was escorted to the royal drawing room of Seraikela Palace, called the Golabandha. Everyone present there knew the story of the conspiracy by the maharaja's father, Dalganjan, which had forever altered the fate of the then Yuvarani of Seraikela, Padmini Kumari. The Yuvarani, however, upon hearing of her uncle's visit, maintained complete decorum, and greeted him respectfully, along with her children—son Tikayet Nripendra Narayan, daughter Ratna Prabha and the two-year-old Pattayet[9] Rajendra. As soon as the child Rajendra saw Maharaja Prithviraj, he sat on his lap and started drumming his head. At any other time, in any other gathering, this would have been interpreted as deeply disrespectful behaviour. As the child continued to play, seated on the Maharaja's lap, everyone watched apprehensively for his reaction. But the Maharaja, it is believed, was impressed by the courage of this bold young prince, who definitely made a lasting impression.

In later years, during a visit of the Duke of Wales in

---

[9]Prince

1921, Prithviraj met Raja Aditya Pratap in Patna and expressed his desire to adopt the Raja's son Rajendra Narayan as his successor.[10] This small interaction altered the course of the history of the princely state of Orissa.

The late Dalganjan's actions were folklore and still fresh in people's minds. Raja Aditya was wary of the notorious conspiratorial atmosphere of the Sailashree Palace, where royal succession to the throne and the power plays involved were usually dangerous. However, after consultation with the royal astrologers, Raja Aditya imposed four conditions: the adoption of Rajendra Narayan should have approval from the central government; both the queens of Prithviraj had to agree to the adoption and be present for the ceremony; the adoption ceremony be held at Sambalpur in the presence of the political agent[11]; the Maharaja of Seraikela, Raja Aditya Pratap Singh Deo, would handpick security personnel for the adopted prince. Raja Aditya Pratap simply could not spare his child without adequate arrangements for his security. This was the reason most of the security arrangements for the young adopted prince came from Seraikela and later, after his marriage with the Patiala princess, from the royal command under the Maharaja of Patiala.

An Adoption and an Inquiry

Many arrangements had to be made for the royal succession; there were chiefs to be invited and rituals to be completed. The official announcement to the government at the Centre, under the British, was made via the political agent assigned to the

---

[10]Though Aditya Pratap had offered both (Tikayet Nripendra Narayan being the other) his sons for adoption, Prithviraj specifically requested for Rajendra.

[11]An officer of the British imperial civil administration legally responsible for the region.

region. The Eastern States Agency[12] had two principal agents at Raipur and Sambalpur, who were directly reporting to the Governor General. While the Raipur agency had the bigger states of Patna and Kalahandi, 23 states, including Seraikela, were under the control of the Sambalpur agency.

The Raja's request to the political agent of Sambalpur to obtain the sanction of the Government of India was met with the response that the adoption was a purely private affair and no official sanction was necessary. The agent, however, assured Aditya Pratap that he would be personally present at the ceremony.

The adoption ceremony took place in the Sonepur Palace, Sambalpur in 1922, in the presence of the political agent, C.L. Philip, Imperial Civil Service (ICS). While the royal family of Seraikela were present, the ranis from Patna were conspicuous by their absence. Soon after the adoption ceremony, Batsraj, who had earlier refused to spare his child, came forward with a claim that Prithviraj had already adopted his son, Bhupal Singh Deo as the successor, for which he had already applied for approval. A controversy erupted, with the destinies of two children at stake. The royal astrologers had already approved and cleared young Rajendra Narayan as the rightful heir, after which the ceremony had taken place. But Batsraj's claim for his son as the legitimate heir to the throne could not be ignored. It necessitated an inquiry at the highest level.

Sir Henry Wheeler, the governor of Bihar and Orissa, was given this task. Adoption and succession have always remained mired in controversy across all royal families of India. After a brief inquiry, Wheeler discovered an important

[12]The Eastern States Agency, created in 1933 during the British rule in India, was a grouping of princely states in eastern India following the unification of the former Chhattisgarh States Agency and the Orissa States Agency that remained intact within the grouping.

document. It was a bill, which showed that Batsraj had borrowed ₹100 from the treasury for the observance of his son Bhupal Singh Deo's birthday. The date was subsequent to his claim of Bhupal's adoption. If the claim of adoption was indeed true, the Maharaja would have observed the birthday of his rightful heir on his own. The technicality disproved Batsraj's claim—had Bhupal indeed been adopted, there would have been no question of borrowing money to celebrate the birthday of the heir to the throne. Batsraj could not explain this technicality and within a short span, the legitimacy of Rajendra Narayan's succession to the throne as its rightful heir was established. The details leading to the investigation by Sir Wheeler remains a mystery till date, as none of the ranis were questioned by the governor's office.

The drama of succession did not end here. On 12 February 1924, Prithviraj Singh collapsed from exhaustion while returning from an elephant hunt. Patna came under the Court of Wards, a standard legal body set up by the East India Company to protect estates when the heir was deemed a minor and was, therefore, incapable of acting independently. The affairs of the state came under a British officer, who was to act on the behalf of the still very young Rajendra Narayan. Around this time, two ranis of Patna came forward and claimed that Batsraj's son Bhupal Deo was the real heir to the throne, justifying the earlier claims, which had already been disproved following the inquiry by Sir Wheeler.

Raja Aditya Pratap, Rajendra Narayan's biological father, was deeply disturbed. On the advice of the governor, he sought the approval of the viceroy of India to officially recognize Rajendra Narayan as the successor to the throne. Following yet another brief investigation, the government finally put the seal of sanction on Rajendra Narayan's succession and the appeal of the ranis was quashed. Rajendra Narayan was just

12 years old when his adoptive father Prithviraj Singh Deo passed away owing to poor health.

Rajendra had a vague apprehension that the controversy over his succession might crop up again. As a student of history, later at school, he understood the implication of the Court of Wards. As he grew up in Seraikela and then at Mayo College in Ajmer and Balangir, he was acutely aware of the uncertainty that was his lot. Ironically, this state of ambiguity left him with a sense of spiritual detachment. He never remained attached to power and position. This consciousness never deserted him.

A SCHOLAR AND SPORTSMAN

Rajendra's early boyhood in Seraikela was punctuated with dance, music, games and sports. He participated in dance and drama for occasional entertainment. He would sing songs with a soft, sweet voice and perform Chhau, a semi-classical dance with movements inspired form martial arts. The royal family had remained patrons of the classical Chhau dance for generations. There are three variations of the Chhau that have survived today—the Seraikela Chhau, the Purulia Chhau and the Mayurbhanj Chhau. While Seraikela and Purulia variations of Chhau use masks during the dance, the Mayurbhanj Chhau does not.

Rajendra's boyhood years were generally spent in revelling in artistic atmosphere until he was enrolled in Mayo College, Ajmer. Mayo has housed many maharajas of the time. Established by Richard Southwell Bourke, sixth earl of Mayo, who served as viceroy of India from 1869 to 1872[13], Mayo College was founded with a view to give the

---

[13]'Richard Southwell Bourke, 6th earl of Mayo', Britannica, 17 February 2022, https://bit.ly/3MbeNDt. Accessed on 4 March 2022.

princely rulers an education along the lines of that at Eton College in Birkshire, England. There was one syllabus, one examination and valuation system for all centres of excellence, modelled after the British system that existed at Eton. The British government had, similarly, set up, all over India, eight institutions known as the Chiefs' Colleges, for the education of princes. One of these, Rajkumar College of Raipur, was nearest to Orissa and would have been a natural choice, but it was ruled out as a security risk. It was conveyed to Seraikela and agreed that Rajendra's education was a sole matter of the Patna State after adoption. Rajendra was thus sent to Mayo College instead. He studied at Mayo from 1922 to 1929.

Rajendra was, at once, a scholar, a sportsman, along with being a Chhau dancer. Throughout his time at school, he was a brilliant student, a class topper and an articulate debater. As an exceptional sportsman, he simultaneously captained various sports teams, including football, hockey, cricket, tennis, table tennis, badminton, even carrom and auction-contract bridge. He also played polo with Himmat Singh and Nagendra Singh, his juniors in college who later became MP and president of the International Court of Justice at The Hague, respectively. Fellow students would call him Raja at college, his colleagues would later address him as Maharaja.

In the examination for getting his diploma, Rajendra ranked first among the students of the Chiefs' Colleges in India in 1929 and was honoured with a gold medal by the viceroy. He was also presented an Austin car by HH Maharajadhiraja Bhupinder Singh of Patiala[14], who was a patron of Mayo College and soon went on to become his father-in-law. The principal of Mayo College at the time, Leslie Jones, wrote

---

[14]Maharaja Bhupinder Singh of Patiala became the first man in the country to own an aircraft, which was bought from the United Kingdom in 1910.

to HH Patiala that he had not seen an equal of Rajendra Narayan in intelligence, conduct and character during his 24 years of experience as a teacher. After Mayo, Rajendra joined St Columba's College, Hazaribag (present-day Jharkhand), and passed his Intermediate Arts examination with flying colours in 1931. Then came the time to get married.

BECOMING KING

Rajendra Narayan was married to Princess Kailash Kumari, daughter of Maharajadhiraja Bhupinder Singh and Maharani Dilip Kaur of Patiala on 24 April 1932. His father-in-law was one of the youngest princes to take an active interest in public affairs after the First World War. The Maharaja of the 17-gun salute state[15] of Patiala would later also serve as the chancellor of the Chamber of Princes, a forum of Indian kings that was set up to voice their needs and aspirations with His Majesty's[16] government. The Chamber also represented the states during the merger discussions with Sardar Patel.

Meanwhile, Patna—declared Court of Wards after the death of Prithviraj—was awaiting its new ruler. It is commonly and quite mistakenly believed that Indian maharajas were not trained into their executive and judicial roles. Many of the rajas from the larger states, after their training at the Chiefs' Colleges[17] went on to study at the erstwhile Prince of Wales Royal Indian

[15]Princely states in British India were granted a gun salute by the British Crown, a protocolary privilege for its ruler to be greeted by a certain number of cannon shots depending upon the size, status and wealth of the state.

[16]Referring to King-Emperor George V.

[17]Chiefs' Colleges, styled on the lines of British public schools, were established to train young Indian princes as leaders and administrators. These colleges were Mayo College, Ajmer; Daly College, Indore; Rajkumar College, Rajkot; Aitchison College, Lahore; Scindia School, Gwalior; Sadul Public School, Bikaner and Hyderabad Public School, Begumpet.

Military College,[18] at Dehradun, or the Royal Military Academy Sandhurst. The smaller kingdoms sent their princes to train at institutions managed by the British government in India. By the time Rajendra completed his administrative training at Ranchi and then at Munghyr, he was 20 years old. The political agent of Sambalpur had administered Balangir from 1924 to 1933 on behalf of the prince. At the age of 21, the young prince would become the absolute ruler of Patna—HH Maharaja Rajendra Narayan Singh Deo.

The formal investiture ceremony was performed on 3 February 1933 in the presence of Sir James David Sifton, Knight Commander of the Indian Empire (KCIE), Knight Commander of the Order of the Star of India (KCSI), Indian Civil Service (ICS), the lieutenant governor of Bihar and Orissa. While installing him on the throne, Sifton enlightened the young ruler on the past progress and future problems of the state and hoped that Patna would take a giant leap forward under the stewardship of the new Maharaja. His address was a glowing tribute to the young Maharaja's talent and temperament:[19]

> It is a source of great pleasure to me that the first visit which I am paying to any of the Orissa states since my appointment as Governor of the Province of Bihar and Orissa should be to Patna State which stands first amongst them in order of precedence. This occasion is one of the greatest importance both to yourself and to the people of your state.
>
> Since your adoption by the late Maharaja Prithviraj Deo in the year 1922 and your succession in the year

[18]Now called Rashtriya Indian Military College.

[19]A copy of the speech from Pabitra Mohan Nayak's personal collection.

1924, my Government has watched your career with the greatest interest and satisfaction. Your academic record gives a strong hope that now you are called to higher and independent responsibility, you will rise to the occasion and display a breadth of vision and devotion to your duties.

Since the death of the late Maharaja Prithviraj Deo, your state has been under the management of Government. During these years its financial resources have been husbanded, (scarce) but notable developments have occurred in all directions and particularly in the matter of medical and educational facilities and in communications. The medical arrangements in Patna State are now exceptionally good. There is also in your state a highly successful child welfare centre which is unique in Orissa. In some areas of the state there is compulsory primary education. The road from Balangir to Sambalpur, and what is likely eventually to be one of the main roads of India, is now open throughout the year that I passed on my way here. I was much impressed by the fine bridges over the Ong and Suktel rivers, which are constructed under the direction of Mr Beckett. A start has also been made with the road which is to connect your headquarters with the new railway line in the west of your state at Katabhanji. At your headquarters, an electrical plant has been installed and a fine new palace has been erected. Your forests are now a source of substantial revenue and I notice with pleasure that a revision is now being carried out of the survey and settlement of your state. The state owes much both to Mr Baldwin, the Superintendent whose death in 1926 was widely regretted and to his successor Mr McGavin.

A great opportunity now lies before you of carrying on and developing the work that has been done in the past. The responsibilities of the ruler of an Indian state

> were never light and at the present time, when each day brings some change, new problems are added to the old. I hope that you will have the wisdom to start slowly and to remember that the present is rooted in the past and that all real progress is continuous. You will always be able to rely on the friendly guidance and assistance of the political officers. It is my confident hope that you will fulfil the promise of your early years and I have no doubt that, if you always place interests of your people before your own, you will be rewarded by their gratitude and by the prosperity and further advancement of your state. It now gives me great pleasure to announce publicly the approval and confirmation by Government of your succession as Ruling Chief of Patna State.

The British had managed to maintain the status quo throughout the time when the administration of Patna State was under the Court of Wards. A new ruler would now take charge of the affairs of his state, which was mired with social evils such as untouchability and child marriage. There was widespread inequality and lack of modern education. Art and handicraft, a traditional strength of the state, remained without direction. The world order was changing. The Industrial Revolution had brought new machines and weapons to the fore. The mighty British Empire, which, at one point, had expanded its control to cover nearly one-fourth of the entire world, had begun to lose its hold over its dominions, protectorates and colonies. Maharaja Rajendra would go on to create an impressive legacy, an administrative order and policy spectrum far ahead of its time and one which would go on to dominate the politics of the region for several generations.

2

A Wise Ruler

It was a turbulent era, when Maharaja Rajendra was installed on the throne of Patna in 1933. At the time, Patna or Patnagarh, as it was also known, was not under direct control of the British Indian government. It was ruled by the maharajas, who administered their own territory under the suzerainty of the British Crown. Balangir was its capital. The name is said to be derived from Balramgarh Fort, built here in the sixteenth century by Balram Deo, the nineteenth raja and founder of Sambalpur. With the Gandhamardan Hills to its northwest and the Tel river to the southeast, Balangir was home to vibrant natural vegetation and wild animals. It also houses many ancient temples of several faiths to this day: Shaivism, Buddhism, Vaishnavism and Tantrism. More importantly, it played a crucial role in the annals of political history of Odisha, both in the pre and post-Independence era.

Patna was then an important part of the Orissa States Agency, alongside Kalahandi, Mayurbhanj and Sonepur as the salute states. Established in 1933, the Eastern States Agency existed for a short period after Independence, after which some of the princely states formed their own Eastern States

Union in 1947,[20] with a strategic vision to establish each state as a self-governing unit within the new Indian Union, with its own finances, judiciary and military. Even this did not last long, given the absence of real political unity among the different Indian states, which was actually the key internal weakness that the British had exploited in their conquest of India. It had taken a foreign conquest from the most powerful empire of its time for the subcontinent to see the advantages of being politically united for a common cause.

A GENTLEMAN OF PRINCIPLES

While India was coming together in its struggle for freedom, the world was reeling under the Great Depression with the destructively expansionist doctrines of Benito Mussolini, Adolf Hitler and Hirohito building up to the Second World War, six years later. In this tumultuous time, imperialism was coming to an end, while the seeds of the freedom struggle in India, sown in the past decades, were growing into a fully-fledged revolution against the British.

The impact of the Great Depression, the dark shadow of the Second World War and the urgency of administrative reform together confronted the young Maharaja. Additionally, prices were rising in the face of economic recession and war. The freedom movement had gathered momentum while the development of the state demanded acceleration. The young ruler was ready to meet these challenges as also rightly specified by the famous scholar, Purna Chandra Rath, the

---

[20]The newly independent India saw the formation of a short-lived Eastern States Union (1947–48) of the princely states. It gathered most of the princely states of the former Orissa Tributary States and Chattisgarh States Agency, with the aim of filling the vacuum of power left behind following the departure of the British.

superintendent of archaeology for the state of Patna, 'Rajendra Narayan was the greatest gift of the late HH Prithviraj to Patna.'[21]

He stood out among all the ruling maharajas of the time, especially for those who expected the young prince to be swayed by wealth, liquor and absolute authority. Rajendra remained a strict monogamist, did not gamble and was a teetotaller. Whenever a drink was offered, he would politely pass it on to his aide-de-camp (ADC)[22]. The poor ADC, in due course of time, turned into an alcoholic. When someone suggested that the ADC must be dismissed on account of his alcoholism, the Maharaja replied, 'The gardener does not uproot the plant he has grown with his own hands.' The ADC was deeply touched and managed to quit drinking with great difficulty.

Unlike other rajas, hunting was not his pastime. When British officers visited the state, the Maharaja used to accompany them into the forest purely out of courtesy being a necessity. He allowed them to see for themselves how the tribal community lived in the deep forest. Unlike the other princes, he simply did not care for hunting.

An interesting anecdote depicting the Maharaja as a gentle but decisive ruler emerges from his work during the land settlement operations in the state. This was the second settlement after 1916, and one of the first steps he undertook as maharaja. The ryots or poor tenant farmers who cultivated the land had no document of ownership with them. The originals were kept in a separate record room with one copy

---

[21]As told to Pabitra Mohan Nayak in a personal interview.

[22]A junior officer, who handles all confidential and private matters of a person holding high rank, usually a senior military officer, is referred to as aide-de-camp or ADC.

called *malik nakal* [copy of the master document] lying with the *gauntia* [the village headman]. Another copy called *ryoti nakal* [copy of the poor tenant farmer] was left with the ryot. The sadar tehsildar was the custodian of records, which were inaccessible to the poor ryots. These were common exploitative realities of the prevalent ryotwari system.

At the time, one Satish Chandra Banerjee, former deputy collector of Bihar and Orissa Province, was the land settlement officer. Rajendra spoke candidly with him, 'See, Banerjee, you are my father's age. You have experience in matters relating to land settlement. I am young and I've no knowledge of settlement work. I solely depend on you. I want you to take up the work impartially and well so that there is no controversy or complaint from the subjects and the interest of the ordinary farmer is not affected.'[23]

Shortly thereafter, a man from Tusra, 30 km south of Balangir, reached the the gate of the palace. He had an axe in his hands and his wife stood beside him. He was shouting against the Maharaja, blaming him for taking away his land, when the Sikh guards stopped him and informed the police. When the Maharaja came to know about this incident, he asked the police not to arrest the man but persuade him to part with the axe. The Maharaja's men were then asked to massage the agitated man's head with oil, give him a cold bath and new clothes to wear. On hearing his plea against the injustice of being parted from his land, the Maharaja asked the settlement officer to keep the records of old and new settlements ready for a spot inspection.

The Maharaja took both the man and his wife in his own car to the attestation camp. He asked the officer to produce a record of the old settlement and enquired if the land in

---

[23]As told to Pabitra Mohan Nayak in a personal interview.

question was sold or mortgaged or gifted. But neither the settlement officer, nor the gauntia could produce any evidence to this effect.

The Maharaja said to the gauntia, 'You are the head of the village, father to the villagers. Grihastha Ashrama[24] dictates that the head of the family must first feed the children, then the pet birds and animals, including other members, before he himself sits down to share his food. But what have you done? You were going to snatch the food from the hands of this tribal, who is your child. Repeat this immoral act and you will be dispossessed.'[25]

He then turned towards Banerjee and said, 'I had given you this responsibility as the settlement officer. You were like my father. But on your account, I was going to be axed. You are yourself a magistrate, first class. Now judge whether your action was right.' Banerjee was both shocked and overwhelmed at the wrath of a king, whose kind and gentle nature he had mistaken for weakness of character. The officer immediately prostrated at his feet, begging for mercy. The man from Tusra burst into tears; his reality changed forever. It took four years (1933–37) to complete the settlement operation.

ALTRUISTIC ADMINISTRATION

The Maharaja, during his reign, insisted that rule of law and conduct go hand in hand. He set aside two days a week—Wednesday and Saturday—for listening to public grievances. He would sit beside a window in the palace with a telephone

[24]As per the Indian tradition, the Grihasta Ashrama refers to the second of the four phases of an individual's life in which he is a householder, being married, begetting children, sustaining one's family and helping support holy persons and fulfilling duties towards gods and ancestors.

[25]As told to Pabitra Mohan Nayak in a personal interview.

and an administrative officer and issue orders on the spot. The Maharaja's oral order was decree. On one instance, the dewan, who was opposed to working women being pregnant, observed that a particular headmistress not be granted maternity leave as she had been with child every year and it was not advisable to continue granting three months leave at a time per annum. Overruling this, the Maharaja ordered that the rules applicable, unless amended, could not debar her from availing a maternity leave with full pay.

Another notable case pertained to a Brahmin widow, Champa, who was deserted by her lover Sripati Guru after when she was three months pregnant. Sripati had joined the ranks of the Utkal Brahman Samaj[26], which had allowed his admission, but rejected Champa's petition for maintenance. The Maharaja agreed with the president of the Samaj in his rejection of Champa's claim to maintenance, but found the presumption of Guru not being the father of Champa's child inadmissible. Consequently, his admission into the Brahmin fold was seen as prejudicial, perverse, immoral and unjust. A woman's entire life and future, along with that of her unborn child, was at stake.

The king ordered this whole matter to be reviewed in a larger Assembly of the Samaj, as there was a great difference of opinions among the members.[27] The Maharaja's noting in this order on case no. 4093D of 1946 is a judicial pronouncement of great social significance: He wrote:

> This case clearly brings out the narrow selfishness of our existing social laws and the one-sided indulgence by males for their own sex and the helplessness of the weaker sex.

[26]The historical caretakers of the Jagannath Temple in Puri.

[27]It was a common act for men in those days to run away from the lover in the garb of becoming a celibate brahmin and remain protected as these women had no means of appeal.

The harshness of the social laws on the weaker sex is so obviously inequitable that one cannot help wondering whether these are laws of a civilized nation or narrow prejudices. The conduct of Sripati has been that of a coward and a beast. I would have admired him as a man, if he had the courage to accept Champa as his wife and her child as his child in spite of what society did or said to him. But instead, he seduced her to satisfy his passion and after impregnating her, deserted her as a coward when he found that the responsibility of parenthood and of having to maintain a family was going to fall on him. Judging from purely moral standards of society to which the parties belong, I should adjudge Champa as innocent. The responsibility of her seduction is entirely on Sripati and he should not escape this moral responsibility. If Champa, whose character is morally on a much higher plane than that of Sripati, has no means of readmission to caste,[28] it will be revolting to all canons of morality, justice and decency, especially if Sripati is allowed to re-enter the caste and is facilitated to avoid his responsibility towards Champa and his child. If people like Sripati find it so easy to re-enter their Samaj, they are only encouraged to repudiate their responsibilities towards poor and helpless girls like Champa.

While all my sympathy goes to Champa, I am afraid I cannot help her in any way under the present social laws of her Samaj. But so far as Sripati's readmission to caste is concerned, I consider the decision of the Samaj perverse, immoral and unjust. It appears that there is a great difference of opinion over this matter amongst members

---

[28]Unwed mothers of the time would be considered as good as expelled from their caste.

> of the Brahmin Samaj and the whole question should be reviewed in a more representative gathering of the Samaj. I accordingly cancel the order of the Brahmin Samaj readmitting Sripati to caste and order that the question may be reconsidered in a more representative meeting of the Samaj.

The judgment demonstrates the deep human sympathy and support he lent to the frail voice of a woman in a patriarchal society.

Meanwhile, his administrative reforms included the constitution of the Patna State Public Service Commission. Constituted in 1940, it ensured that qualities, as well as qualifications were key to one's entry into a permanent job. The committee decided on matters of retirement, pensions, allowances, provident fund, holidays, travel allowance, promotion, punishment, etc. A 'civil list' of employees with pay scales above ₹40 was annually published. The history of service of gazetted officers was systematically and regularly maintained along with appropriate service records of non-gazetted employees. Whenever there was a need to introduce a new regulation, the Public Service Regulations prevalent in British India were followed.

The Maharaja undertook a number of measures to organize administration on modern lines. He ran the state through a Cabinet and an Assembly. The various functions of governance were divided among different departments, which remained under the charge of ministers. The ministry[29] worked objectively, with impartiality and transparency. The Cabinet members consisted of Raj Bahadur Kanwar as his CM. Noted lawyer Gopal Chandra was his minister for home

---

[29]The entire administration under the Maharaja.

and development. Laxman Sahani was his revenue minister and Ranendra Singh Deo functioned as his chief secretary. The Maharaja's CM functioned like a vice president who presided over Cabinet meetings in his absence. His entire Cabinet and staff consisted of decorated officers functioning under the singular authority of the Maharaja. Incidentally, even Maharaja Bhupinder, his father-in-law had a singular, secular Cabinet in his state with a Muslim as his PM,[30] a Sikh as the home minister, a Hindu as the law minister, an Englishman as the finance minister and a scholarly Keralite for foreign minister. Similarly, Rajendra's ministers hailed from different provinces like Uttar Pradesh (UP), Rajasthan, Bengal and Orissa. In due course, his administration was at least 10 years ahead of British Orissa in every field. He was an efficient ruler who was sensitive to the needs of his people.

JUDICIAL TRANSFORMATION

Rajendra believed in the independence of the judiciary. He instructed the judicial system to function with compassion. Death sentence in Patna was converted to life imprisonment. As Maharaja, in a notable initiative of his time, he separated the executive from the judiciary. At the time, India had a federal court. The apex court came much later. Rajendra adopted the pattern of the judicial commission and the federal court. On 6 September 1940, he established a high court of judicature in Balangir with the power to review judicial and criminal cases. The high court consisted of one chief justice, two justices and one registrar. The judicial committee comprised Kanwar, Chandra and Sahani. The Maharaja was the appellate authority with the power to grant pardon.

[30]The PM in the Patiala Darbaar reported directly to the Maharaja.

At the lower level, the sub-divisional officer (SDO), tehsildar and the tax inspector were relieved from judging cases. Then there was the munsiff[31] or the magistrate and the sub-judge, who worked under the civil and sessions judge in 1943. S.C. Chakravarti was the civil and sessions judge at the time. Till today, Balangir enjoys the special privilege of the district and sessions court and its district judge accepts appeals to the high court as registrar. This has allowed Balangir to lay a moral claim for the establishment of a bench of the Orissa High Court.

British author E.M. Forster in his essay 'India Again' in *Two Cheers for Democracy* wrote about the typical Indian attitude of hero-worship. Indians, he says, are either uncritical or overcritical. To their eyes, a man is either a god or a devil. Yet, the Maharaja was more than ordinary, and this became even more evident as he got older. He was head and shoulders above the common run of rajas and zamindars, and better known by his accomplishments, rather than lineage. The Maharaja did for Patna, in less than 15 years, what many other Garjat rajas had not been able to accomplish in half a century.

SOCIAL MAKEOVER

In 1933, Patna remained a tribal-dominated forest tract, with a superstitious society. For assisting a society plagued by untouchability, obstinacy and short sightedness, challenges undoubtedly had to be converted into opportunity. Rajendra had long believed that 'if man was indeed the temple of the

[31]The munsiff was the judge and presiding officer of the district in charge of all the tax inspectors (tehsildars).

living God, there was no place for discrimination'.[32]

The untouchables or Harijans were the most despised and deprived community in Patna, as elsewhere in the country. In those days, the Brahmins believed that even the shadow of a Harijan could defile them, and thus, they were banished from entering temples for worship. Some of the rulers enabled this. The Maharaja, on the other hand, welcomed the Harijans into Patna. Their entry into Hindu temples was the first step towards legitimizing their rights. Raghunath Temple, the main palace temple, was the first to open its doors to the 'untouchables'. The shift in the perception and the eventual eradication of untouchability from the princely states was initiated by the Sailashree Palace opening its doors to the Harijans. The Maharaja claimed this on record: 'Perhaps, I was the first ruler in India to remove untouchability and allow temple entry to Harijans in my state, convinced of Gandhiji's viewpoints long before it was implemented in the rest of the country through legal legislation and constitutional provisions.'[33]

Another social evil prevalent amid Garjats was child marriage. This grotesque violation of human rights was prevalent across India and deeply embedded in society. For the Maharaja, this proved to be a more complex task than opening the temple gates in his capacity as absolute ruler. To avoid revulsion and resentment, a consensus needed to be achieved among village heads. A conference of pandits was organized, which was attended by learned scholars from Puri and Cuttack. It took three days and prolonged debates

---

[32]Mentioned in Maharaja's private diary.

[33]The decision was made by royal decree and was recorded in an affidavit submitted by the Maharaja to the government of India during accession. The affidavit exists as a private record copy with the royal family in Patna.

to arrive at a resolution to permit only adult marriages across the Garjats.

The Maharaja believed in the rule of law. Yet, being of a democratic viewpoint, he understood that the law should not be imposed on the people, but should come from them. Therefore, Patna, during his tenure, saw a combination of progress and peace. His government was the people's government.

FARM REFORMS

In 1944, the Maharaja did away with the office of the sadar tehsildar as the custodian of records and created a land records department. Around 300 cooperative banks and societies were commissioned to provide easy loans to farmers. The Maharaja also established an agriculture school to which students came from other Garjats. The affairs of the Department of Agriculture were taken away from the revenue minister and put under the direct charge of the chief secretary. An able officer named Amarnath Kohli was appointed as the chief agriculture officer.

The farmers who used to sit idle for four months a year were now engaged in summer cultivation. The use of green manure was encouraged. Compost manure from leaves, weeds and bushes was prepared. Some farmers were even sent to Raipur for a month's training in compost preparation. High-yield wheat was obtained from imperial botanical gardens and distributed among cultivators. Tobacco and South Kosala cotton (a variety of fine cotton) was cultivated on the black soil of the state. Under the new agricultural reforms, the Maharaja established an agriculture farm on 140 acres of land, of which 40 acres was earmarked for preparation of green manure. Farmers were trained to grow more grains. Rajendra Experimental Farm was set up to train students in the science of cultivation. The farm started cultivation of vegetables and fruits. Hybrid cattle were maintained to supply milk and a dairy farm was established. Bulls were imported from Sindh.[34] The Grow More Food Scheme of the central government was adopted. Gaushalas or cow-shelters were set up for cattle care. No longer would old, sick, blind or lame cattle be let off on the road because it had outlived its utility.

An agricultural research centre was also raised at Larkipali near Balangir. Horticulture experts were engaged for the development of gardens and orchards. A chicken farm and a cattle farm with hybrid variety were established, offering provision of 200 acres of pasture. A library was set up with books on agriculture. Articles on model farming were published in the *Patna Dipika*, for free distribution among farmers. Pamphlets on insects and crop diseases were published and propagated. Modern granaries for the preservation of grains were also set up. Steps for crop preservation were initiated. An agriculture officer was deputed to the Imperial Agricultural Research Institute[35] for short-term training. An agricultural exhibition was organized every year. Farmers form Patna were sent to participate in agricultural exhibitions organized in different states.

Patna State, under the reign of Maharaja, with its democratic set-up and welfare measures was far ahead of its time. For instance, Maharaja announced the promulgation of local self-government through panchayats. This was the beginning of Patna State Gram Panchayat Law of 1939, well before the panchayat system was enshrined in Article 40 of the Indian constitution.

---

[34]The Red Sindh Bull is a reputed heat-tolerant milch cattle breed originating from Sindh province of what is now Pakistan.

[35]Now known as the Indian Agricultural Research Institute (IARI) at Pusa Road, New Delhi.

Several years later, following deep popular discontent against the first Five-Year Plan, Jawaharlal Nehru constituted the Team for the Study of Community Projects and National Extension Service in 1957 to examine the working of the Community Development Programme, which was launched in 1952. Headed by the venerable Balwantrai Mehta, an eminent parliamentarian who later became the CM of Gujarat, the committee, which came to be popularly known as Balwantrai Mehta Committee, recommended a local system of governance for villages in rural India. It also recommended the establishment of a three-tier panchayati raj system with a gram panchayat at the village level and the panchayat samiti and district parishad at the block and district levels, respectively. The Government of India accepted these recommendations for implementation on 26 January 1961. There were 300 gram panchayats for Sadar villages[36], 260 for Titilagarh and 210 for Patnagarh, totalling to 770 in all. Each panchayat with tenure of three years had five to 11 elected members.[37] Its duty was to look after the cleanliness of the village, distribution of water for irrigation and primary education, along with maintenance of tanks and drains, village roads, temples and *deraghar* or the village guest house.

The state of Patna, however, had already implemented this reform well before the Government of India realized its importance. In 1943, the Maharaja had established praja sabhas, one each in Balangir, Titlagarh and Patnagarh. It advised the government on matters of development and was guided by praja sabha rules of Patna State. From gram panchayats in villages to praja sabha in towns, the Maharaja expanded the introduction of self-rule in his state.

---

[36]'Sadar' is an archaic Hindustani word for 'tehsil'.

[37]https://bit.ly/3khpusm. Accessed on 28 April 2022.

Additionally, he implemented sweeping reforms in the land revenue system and restoration of tenants' rights through a tenancy act to allow the rule of law to prevail. He divided the state into three revenue sub-divisions: Balangir Sadar, Titlagarh and Patnagarh. The Patna State Tenancy Act, 1944, was promulgated to amend and consolidate the law relating to agricultural tenancies in Patna State. The whims and caprices of subordinate officers no longer decided the destiny of farmers. Despite a setback in revenue collection in 1938 and 1940 on account of inclement weather conditions and consequent crop failure, the revenue of the state increased more than threefold in 12 years.

DEVELOPMENT WORKS

Other sectors like transport, communication, health, education, trade and public works also flourished during the tenure of the new Maharaja. In the early 1940s, a state transport corporation was set up, the first of its kind in Orissa, to provide bus services to the people. Sometimes called Kosal Transport, it ran buses from Balangir to the sub-divisional headquarters, even to Sonepur and Bargarht—a distance of about 80 km—where the body of buses was manufactured locally and exported. There were buses plying from Balangir to Bileisarda, Kudasinga, Bandhpara and Desand. Later, the Orissa Road Transport was set up at Berhampur. While Patna State Transport buses were red in colour, Orissa Road Transport buses were painted grey. Road transport remained under a general manager, while state transport worked under the Orissa governor. It was merged into what is today known as the Orissa State Road Transport Corporation.

For development works, the Maharaja established Kosala Development Syndicate. The engine house in the capital town, which supplied electricity to Sailashree Palace, was extended to supply electricity to the town. Further, to shorten distances and connect his people, roads were aligned and bridges were built at a time when Sonepur had no bridges. The Kukuda jor[38] between Balangir and Sonepur had a causeway, but no bridge—the jors and rivers from Balangir to Titilagarh were bridged, and new ones were constructed over Ong and Suktel. The foundation of the Tel bridge was laid much later during the Maharaja's tenure as CM.

The Maharaja also focused on plantation and afforestation. Jamun and neem trees lined the roads in Patna State. A designated day to celebrate and worship the forests was observed in Patna State back in 1934, perhaps the first of its kind in the country.[39] These works demonstrate the Maharaja as an environmentalist.

In the field of healthcare, the Maharaja established a fully equipped hospital with an electrotherapy institute in which an X-ray machine from Germany, one of the only three in the country at the time, was installed in 1935—which marked the silver jubilee year of George V becoming the emperor of India. This period also saw the establishment of eye and leprosy hospital. Provisions were made at Balangir, Loisingha and Patnagarh for the treatment of rabies. A maternity centre for safe delivery was also established.

The Maharaja set up hospitals in Patnagarh, Kantabanji, Tusra and Belpada besides three dispensaries covering the areas of Agalpur, Khaprakhol, Turekela, Tikrapara and Sindhekela. He also founded two child welfare centres. There were trained pharmacists, nurses and doctors for women. Health visitors

---

[38]Jors are small nallahs that stream into a river.

[39]Kanaiyalal Maneklal Munshi later popularized this practice by planting a tree at Rajghat, Delhi, in 1950. The celebration is now known as Van Mahotsava.

and nurses were engaged to help pregnant women in villages through labour and delivery. The Maharaja, perhaps, knew about the history of Chauhan rulers of Patna: for the safe delivery of Narasingha Deva's rani, his younger brother Balaram Dev was sent across the Ong in high flood to get an expert nurse from Sonepur. As a reward for this daring adventure, Narasingh Deva presented Balaram with the territory left to the Ong, which later became the Sambalpur tract.

He even established an Ayurveda hospital named after Sarada Devi—a disciple of the yogi and spiritual guru, Ramakrishna Paramahamsa—with a network of Ayurvedic dispensaries all over the state.

EDUCATION FOR SELF-RELIANCE

The Maharaja introduced various measures for spreading education in his state. Due importance was given to female education and schools were established especially for girls. In 1941, he announced compulsory and free primary education for boys and girls aged six to 11 years. There were 57 primary schools, 28 schools for girls, three high schools and two teacher training schools. There was one examination board for the entire state. Students were taught physical education, leadership, dutifulness, cleanliness, thrift and self-reliance. They also cleaned roads, tanks, drains and hospital premises, and distributed food among patients. When renowned poet and social reformer Pt Godabarish Mishra met the Maharaja in 1944 and requested him to set up a college to provide higher education to boost the infrastructure of Utkal University, he immediately responded. Rajendra College of Arts and Commerce, affiliated with Utkal University, was established in the same year; it was the first college among the 24 Garjats and the first commerce college in Orissa. The second college came up in Baripada four years later in 1948 in the name of Purna Chandra Bhanj Deo, the first pro-chancellor of Utkal University.

Rajendra College was started in a military barrack owing to its pending construction. Foreign engineers had prepared a blueprint for a circular college building 350 km away at Manoharpur, with flower gardens, grasslands, staff-quarters around the hostel building, a playground, a swimming pool and a college hall decked with pieces of art. A construction committee was constituted and it went around Allahabad University, Lucknow University, Calcutta University and Banaras Hindu University seeking inspiration for creating a world-class institution. The committee submitted its report, but unfortunately, construction could not be implemented on account of the merger of the princely states with the Dominion of India. Rajendra College stands as Rajendra (Autonomous) College in Balangir today. The Annapurna Orphanage, also established by the Maharaja, was run by a committee of 12 persons, five government officials and seven private members. Stipends were given to meritorious children for higher studies.

By 1944, as a result of the Second World War, India was experiencing an acute shortage of paper. Students were asked to use pencils and reuse paper after having erased whatever they had previously written. Oral tests were conducted to make up for the deficit of paper.

Contrarily, however, there was no shortage of paper in Patna that had a handmade paper plant. Even government forms and circulatory literature such as the *Patna Dipika* was printed on handmade paper. Inspired by Mahatma Gandhi, the Maharaja had sought to cultivate self-reliance. There were charkhas in every school. Students worked these charkhas to spin thread that was sold. The sales proceeds were used to develop school gardens and financially support the poor students. The Maharaja also inaugurated an Rajendra Institute of Economic Research on 20 November 1945.[40] It trained college students in the collection of statistics on the basis of which post-war reconstruction work was taken up. The institute was envisaged to eventually become the nerve centre of the Eastern States Agency and a regional centre for economic development. However, it remained an unrealized dream due to the merger.

Well-connected with the outside world through telegraph and telephone, Balangir became an education hub. Industrial and technical schools were started in Patna State. There was a carpentry school and a school for blacksmiths. To meet the fallout of the Second World War, public works were undertaken that led to the construction of a graphite plant, a match factory, a tile factory, a rice mill besides a unit of filigree work, all of which were set up to widen the scope of employment. A leather factory in Titilagarh was also established. Post Independence, it came to be known as the Orissa Leather Corporation.

The Maharaja started the Patna State weaving industry under the textiles department: door screens and bedsheets made here were exported; there were 55 looms and a sewing department. A trade syndicate was established in 1946 to control and monitor trade in the state.

A PEOPLE'S KING

Rajendra Narayan was a secular Hindu, who had learnt tantra, an often discreet esoteric practice among Indian rulers and politicians, even today. Patna, being one of the seats of tantra, was one of the reasons the Maharaja worshipped the seven tantric sisters namely Jnanadei Maluni, Sua Teluni, Nitai Dhobani, Gangi Gauduni, Sukuti Chamaruni, Luhukuti

[40] *Modern Review*, Vol. 79, Issue 5, Taylor and Francis, 1946.

Luhurani and Patrapindhi Saurani, highly revered in Puri. The tantric rituals practised by the Maharaja were intended for the well-being of mankind. As a result of his conscientious and disciplined approach to tantra, he acquired a rare ability to cure snake bites through a mantra, a fable which became popular across the state. In addition to the regular telegrams, the Maharaja also received many from his citizens who had suffered snakebites. His mail was segregated as official, personal and snakebite letters. He would then collect all the snakebite telegrams, read out his mantras and the people who had sent them would be miraculously cured. This was tried and tested across his subjects. The Maharaja's spiritual abilities were well-known to his citizens. Yet, he remained a secular ruler. He would organize a *Vishnu Yagna* at Balangir. He also encouraged people of the Christian faith to build a church in town.

In his relationship with his subordinates, the Maharaja was tolerant and understanding. The extreme outburst of his displeasure only included, 'Why did you do this?' His smiling face instilled confidence and a sense of security. His humility, his friendliness, his refinement and culture made him an ideal maharaja.

In the orchard behind the Sailashree Palace, the Maharaja would often see the crop in abundance, but the fruits would somehow vanish from the trees. He would often wonder where and how they disappeared.

One day, while on the terrace, he spotted an individual climb one of the trees and run away with ripe mangoes. This alerted the Maharaja. He possessed a movie camera with a powerful lens. He began recording and taking pictures of guards and strangers often visiting the garden to steal the fruits. He also managed to record the palace guards asleep in their chairs during duty hours. Soon, the palace staff was invited to watch a film, for which they were excited. Through the film, a message was silently and brilliantly conveyed. The effect was remarkable. Dereliction of duty became a thing of the past, including thefts from the orchards and gardens. No one lost their job. No case was reported to the police.

Nilamani Senapati, ICS, and also the chief administrator of the Garjats remembers the Maharaja in his writings: 'A ruling chief during British days had full powers over his subjects. Rajendra Narayan made no use of those powers for his personal benefit very unlike many rajas and maharajas. In fact, I found Patna better administered than most British districts.'[41]

The Maharaja's vision and able leadership resulted in rapid progress in transport, communication, education and healthcare industry, winning him the respect of his peers and the British government, which honoured him with the title of KCIE. He was given the title 'HH' and was received with a nine-gun salute until India's independence and the merger of the Indian princely states, in which the Maharaja had a key role to play.

---

[41]Senapati, Nilamani, *Orissa District Gazetters*, Orissa Government Press, Cuttack, 1968.

3

The Merger

India's freedom movement against the British underwent an ideological evolution stretching from a demand for self-rule to complete independence, which was not on the agenda until 1942, when Mahatma Gandhi launched the Quit India Movement in Bombay. This can be inferred from the report by the Nehru Committee, submitted to the All Parties Conference in 1928, which had then demanded self-government under dominion status[42] within the empire.[43] This committee was headed by Pandit Motilal Nehru—with his son Jawaharlal acting as his secretary—and consisted of nine other members. Within a year, discontentment brewed and the political climate had changed. Following the increasingly violent regional movements that demanded complete sovereignty, a resolution was passed in the Lahore session of the Congress in 1929 demanding complete or Purna Swaraj, followed by a civil disobedience movement throughout the country. Historical

[42]Dominions were the semi-independent polities under the British Crown that constituted the British Empire.

[43]'Nehru Report (Motilal Nehru, 1928)', Constitution of India, https://bit.ly/3ud769D. Accessed on 6 April 2022.

markers suggest that until the Nehru Committee Report of 1928, the Indian National Congress (INC) had had no definite approach to the princely states that occupied about 40 per cent of India's territory.

On 8 August 1942, Mahatma Gandhi's Quit India Movement called for the complete withdrawal of the British. However, in the midst of the Second World War, PM Winston Churchill remained adamant that independence could only be a matter of discussion after the war, which was at its turning point. With global attention on the World War, there was poor international support for India's freedom movement, and the support from the Americans could best be described as lukewarm. Even Indian royalty did not have much faith in the movement barring a few like Rajkumari Amrit Kaur of Kapurthala, who even participated in the freedom struggle and fully supported it. Other princes sided with the British.

Amidst British reluctance to initiate talks of granting administrative control to the Indians, Earl Archibald Percival Wavell (then Commander-in-Chief, India, Lord Wavell), the viceroy of India, eventually managed to trigger negotiations and facilitated a serious dialogue. Although Churchill was openly hostile towards the idea of independence, his successor, Clement Attlee, who became the British PM in 1945, was more sympathetic and drastically altered British policy.

Wavell was no politician; he had served on the frontline and led the British forces to victory over the Italians in Egypt and Libya as commander-in-chief of the Middle East till 1941. Within two weeks of assuming office, he ordered the military to assist in the supply of food and medicines to address the Bengal famine of 1943. This was a notable departure from the policy adopted by his predecessor, Victor Hope, second marquess of Linlithgow. By 1945, times were beginning to change; Radio Hamburg had announced the death of Adolf Hitler on 1 May.

This allowed the Indian viceroy to reaffirm his government's determination to grant self-government and hope that the political leaders of India would assume ministerial positions in the future.[44] Wavell's contribution to the independence debate, especially the setting up of a timetable for withdrawal, remains one of the key turning points in British Indian history. The destiny of the Indian princes would be altered forever in the coming years.

SINK OR SWIM?

Even as the expectation of independence became a certainty, Rajendra Narayan could anticipate the future and the challenges in store for the princely states. As a member of the Chamber of Princes, it was clear to him that when the British left, they would take away their support system, leaving the rulers at the mercy of the people they ruled.

The freedom struggle had kindled a people's movement, which had begun to openly challenge the rulers and aristocrats of all princely states. People in the princely states were demanding the abolition of taxes and the establishment of responsible government. The conglomeration of political movements in the princely states came to be known as the Praja Mandal movements. For instance, in July 1931, the third annual conference of the Punjab Riyasti Praja Mandal in Shimla had demanded the deposition of Rajendra Narayan's father-in-law, the Maharaja of Patiala.[45] The praja mandals were naturally allied with the Congress, given their democratic

[44]Menon, V.P., *The Story of the Integration of the Indian States,* Bombay, Orient Longmans, 1956.

[45]'Panjab Riyasti Praja Mandal', *The Sikh Encyclopedia,* https://bit.ly/3KZtp8l. Accessed on 21 March 2022.

set-up. The Congress too had started taking an interest in the native states by 1936, its policy being to heed the demand of self-determination of the people of the princely states.

Some Congress leaders in Orissa began to encourage the people to demand freedom not only from the British, but the rulers as well. The reality of an independent India with princely states forming a united political unit was not acceptable. The Congress, therefore, supported the praja mandals and played a key role in the revival of the defunct Garjat Praja Sammilani, a united front in Orissa against the ruling chiefs. To face the challenges posed by the praja mandals, the British had proposed that the ruling chiefs form an organization of their own.

Maharaja Rajendra understood that times were changing and within a short period, the people would become the rulers in an era of democracy. There was, therefore, an urgent need for the rulers to discuss how they were going to deal with the new situation.

While most of the rajas and maharajas were unconcerned about the storm brewing in the political horizon of the country, there were some from states like Mayurbhanj and Patna, who were seriously seized with the problems ahead. This is clear from the letters the Maharaja of Mayurbhanj wrote—just one year before the merger—to the Maharawal[46] of Dungarpur and to the Nawab Hamidullah Khan of Bhopal. On 9 May 1946, Mayurbhanj Maharaja, Sir Pratap Chandra Bhanj Deo, confessed in his letter to the ruler of Dungarpur: 'We are nothing but anachronisms and feudalistic relics to the vast majority of our politically-minded countrymen. Congress leader Harekrushna Mahatab[47] calls us the third line of defence

[46]A titular head like Maharaja.

[47]Harekrushna Mahatab was a leader of the INC, who went on to become the first CM of Orissa from 1946-50 and then from 1956-60.

for British imperialism. Had it not been for us, the British rule would have long ago crumbled in India.'[48]

The Maharaja of Mayurbhanj also wrote a letter to Nawab Muhammad Hamidullah Khan Bahadur of Bhopal on 19 September 1946 that contained a message that rang loud and clear to the rulers of India:[49]

> The rulers have come to depend more and more upon the support of the paramount power and less and less on the support of their people. One result of the British policy towards Indian states, whether deliberately intended or not, has been to undermine the authority of the rulers over their people. Our people have thus been gradually alienated from us. The British have painted us as mischievous relics of an archaic system. The main prop of our existence is now being withdrawn, a necessary evil to be got rid of in more favourable circumstances. The rulers may even be acclaimed as heroes who by an unprecedented act of self-sacrifice, have made valuable contributions to a permanent solution of a complicated political problem. If, on the other hand, we cling to our so-called sovereign rights and continue in a career constantly bickering with our people and British India, a renunciation of this character should be forced upon us in far less pleasant circumstances. By postponing the evil today, we may merely be denying ourselves the chances of an honourable exit from the state, because when it comes about at a later date, our exit may well have the appearance of ignominious dismissal with a new government in British India responsible to an Indian legislature.

[48]In a letter written to the ruler of Dungarpur by Mayurbhanj Maharaja, Sir Pratap Chandra Bhanj Deo.

[49]Private records of Sailashree Palace.

In as early as 1943, Rajendra invited the rajas and maharajas of Orissa and Chhattisgarh Garjats to a conference at Sailashree Palace, Balangir. The political agent of Sambalpur, was also invited to join the deliberations. The purpose of this meet was to discuss the future of the princely states following British withdrawal.

Initially, the rajas could not fully acknowledge the gravity of the situation. After the forenoon session, they were largely gossiping when Maharaja Rajendra Narayan hurtled into the gathering and proclaimed that it was no time for idle talk. It was a life and death question for the rulers. They needed to ask themselves why they had been invited to the conference. What was going to happen to them and to their successors who were being provided an expensive education tailored to make them fit for the throne. It was only a matter of time before the states and status would slip away from their hands after the British would quit India. As for himself, the Maharaja observed, that he had prepared himself to manage within his means. 'But what about you?' he asked strongly. The rajas were stunned but convinced. The Orissa rulers could conceive the gravity of the inevitable hurtling towards them.

Change was certainly on the cards and Rajendra Narayan already had the vision of two divisions of Odia states: firstly, Seraikela-Kharsawan with the new state of Orissa, and secondly, a separate region comprising Garjats, along with Bastar, Deobhog, Phuljhar, Sakti and Sarangarh. This could have eventually paved the path for a greater and more influential Orissa than it is in today's political landscape. Possibly, Odia could have stood out as a language apart from Hindi, to govern more than one state. But this was not to be.

Unlike the Maharaja, Congress leader Mahatab favoured the merger of 26 Odia-speaking princely states with the Orissa Province and a single administration for both the states and the province. As president of the State People's Enquiry Committee, that submitted its report in 1939, Mahatab had recommended the withdrawal of state support for the princely states and their merger with Orissa Province. He observed in the report that once the Garjats merge with Orissa, all their problems could be resolved.

It was becoming increasingly evident to the princes that following British withdrawal, it would not be possible for them to continue enjoying the security and privilege that they once did. In June 1946, on the eve of the transfer of power, when the Chamber of Princes met in the Conference Hall of the Taj Mahal Palace Hotel in Mumbai, Rajendra Narayan opined that they could either sink or swim in India. He suggested that the princely states should accede to India by subordinating all personal interest.

BUILD-UP TO INDEPENDENCE

Closer to India's independence, the Congress had distanced itself from the praja mandals and decided to work alongside the princely states to develop governance strategies following the transfer of power. In March 1946, Britain had despatched a Cabinet Mission to India, aimed to discuss the transfer of power from the British government to the Indian leadership consisting of members of the Congress and the Muslim League, headed by Mohammed Ali Jinnah. The aim of the mission was to settle with the leaders and arrive at an acceptable procedure for framing a new constitutional structure for India. Mahatma Gandhi and Jinnah had both written to each other in the run-up to the Cabinet Mission, in order to reach a settlement between the Congress and the Muslim League, and effectively clear any internal roadblocks to Independence. But these talks had failed.

In the meantime, Wavell had assured the princely states that without their consent, no changes would be made in the relationship between the Indian princes and the British Crown on the question of the rights guaranteed to them.[50] The only suggestion was that they must reform their administration on modern lines for the welfare of their subjects. The Chamber of Princes had welcomed both the assurance and the suggestion. However, the new Labour government led by PM Clement Attlee, in subsequent decisions, made it clear that the princes were more or less on their own, which was becoming increasingly evident to the princely states.

The Cabinet Mission invited the princely states for a discussion about the future, and was attended by the rulers of Bhopal, Patiala, Bikaner, Dungarpur and Bilaspur. The states of Hyderabad, Travancore and Jaipur were represented in these discussions by their dewans—Nawab Muhammad Ahmed Said Khan of Chhatari, Sir C.P. Ramaswami Iyer and Sir Mirza Ismail, respectively. The nawab of Bhopal had made it clear that the rulers wished to continue with a maximum degree of sovereignty, even if it meant being grouped into larger regional units. The Mission, on their part, made it clear that if British India were granted independence, it would also mean the end of treaty obligations with the Indian states. It was a stalemate. The Mission's consultations with the states and subsequently with the Indian political leadership were equally inconsequential. The Congress and the Muslim League were not inclined to compromise.

On 16 May 1946, the Cabinet Mission concluded that there should be a Union of India comprising both British India provinces and the Indian states. Over portfolios, like foreign

---

[50]Chamber of Princes, India. *Proceedings of the meetings of the Chamber of Princes (Narendra Mandal),* Government of India Press, 1940–46.

affairs, defence, finance and communication, the Centre would have exclusive jurisdiction. It proposed the separation of powers between an executive and legislature, consisting of individuals from British India and the state representatives. The Mission theorized the Indian map into a complicated division of three principal sections; the Centre, the regional groups and the provinces of British India. However, the plan failed to arrive at a consensus on the question of having Muslim-majority and Hindu-majority provinces balanced at the central legislature.

Jinnah wanted the zones comprising Bengal and Assam in the Northeast, Punjab, the North-West Frontier Province, Sind and Baluchistan to be constituted into a sovereign, independent state of Pakistan. He remained adamant in all meetings where Mahatma Gandhi had requested the support of the Muslim League till independence, after which the question of Pakistan would have been put to the table. He unequivocally called for Pakistan to be created alongside India. The talks failed.

By then, the British had begun to clearly see that their influence within India and its leaders was rapidly beginning to diminish. In a sweeping decision, the British sided with the Congress and decided to invite Nehru to be sworn in as the PM of an interim government on 12 August 1946. The British assumed that Jinnah would eventually back down from his demand for Pakistan and join Nehru's Cabinet. Jinnah however, refused to join the interim government and the Muslim League reacted violently[51] four days after the decision of electing an interim government and ignoring their demand for Pakistan.

---

[51]Jinnah had announced Direct Action Day on 16 August 1946 that led to widespread communal killings in Calcutta under the charge of the Muslim League CM Huseyn Shaheed Suhrawardy.

The dissent by the Muslim League did not prevent Lord Wavell from going ahead and swearing in Nehru's interim Cabinet on 2 September 1946. The Constituent Assembly of India was also inaugurated, which boycotted the Muslim League entirely.

Meanwhile, the Indian rulers too were watching the Cabinet Mission carefully. The Chamber of Princes had met several times after their deliberations with the Mission. The Indian states had resolved that the entry of the states into the Union would be based on thorough negotiations and the final decision would lie with each state. The Union could not interfere in the administrative matters of the states. The nawab of Bhopal reiterated that there would be some satisfactory assurances required before the majority[52] of states could join the Constituent Assembly. As no acceptable solution seemed to be in sight, the Indian states adopted a wait-and-watch strategy.[53]

The impasse continued. By 1947, given the failure of the talks and the prolonged stalemate, PM Attlee lost confidence in Lord Wavell. Lord Louis Mountbatten of Burma was installed as the next and last viceroy of India. The appointment was followed by a declaration that the British would quit India within a year.[54] It was only a matter of time before the history and geopolitical balance of Asia would be altered forever.

THE MOUNTBATTEN PLAN

Upon his arrival, Mountbatten sought approval for a revised version of the original Cabinet Mission plan. The new plan

---

[52]The states of Baroda and Cochin had openly expressed their willingness to join the Constituent Assembly without any assurances.

[53]The Maharajas of Bikaner and Patiala openly dissented against a wait-and-watch strategy.

[54]It was declared that the transfer of power would be concluded by June 1948.

stated that independence would be granted to the provinces of British India and the Indian states, and then they could choose to get together or remain sovereign in whichever way they wanted, putting everyone on an equal footing. The British had now succeeded in creating a complete mess in their hurry to transfer power. Nehru rejected this proposal outright; it would have led to Balkanization of the subcontinent. Facing the disastrous consequences of the new plan, both Nehru and Jinnah pressed for a separate Pakistan seeing this as the only way out of this stalemate. Sensing consensus and an end to the impasse, Mountbatten announced the formation of a Hindu-majority dominion of India and a Muslim-majority dominion of Pakistan, with the new boundary lines to be kept secret until the inauguration of the new dominions.

On 3 June 1947, Mountbatten announced the final decision of the British government, which would transfer powers to two dominions of India and Pakistan. The Congress and the Muslim League both accepted this decision within a few days of the announcement. Interestingly, the position of the princely states in the Mountbatten Plan was left unchanged: that is, with the ending of the paramountcy they could join either grouping or proclaim their independence and establish their separate relations with Britain. The Plan stated, 'The princes' states, covering two-fifths of the area of India with a population of 93 million would join one or other federation, or possibly, in the case of one or two larger States, such as Hyderabad and Travancore, according to their present declared intentions, proclaim their separate independence.[55]

Mountbatten made it clear to the princely states that His Majesty's government would not confer dominion status

---

[55]Dutt, R. Palme, *The Mountbatten Plan For India,* Labour Monthly, The Labour Publishing Company Ltd, London, 1947, pp. 210-19, https://bit.ly/36ZreTZ. Accessed on 7 March 2022.

to any state that wished to remain independent of India or Pakistan. It was clear that the British were adamant on leaving and the Indian rulers would have to decide their fate amongst themselves. By this time, the states of Baroda, Bikaner, Cochin, Jaipur, Patiala and Rewa had decided to send their representatives to the Constituent Assembly. The short-lived unity among the Indian princes as well as their institutional set-up, the Chamber of Princes, would come to an abrupt end with the exit of the British in August 1947. Many Indian rulers held the opinion that the Chamber should have been replaced with a new organization. Indian royalty, on the brink of finding political unity for the first time in the history of the subcontinent, fell back into the old ways where each state would pay attention to their own vested interests.

The Mountbatten Plan fast-tracked the process and the two nations were created on 14 and 15 August in the same year. The dates were separated by a day in order to ensure Mountbatten would be able to attend both ceremonies. Jinnah achieved his long-standing wish to become the *Quaid-e-Azam* of Pakistan, a theocratic state.

Nehru would become the PM of India. As per the Congress strategy, Sardar Patel was given charge of the department of states. This was a wise decision. There existed serious differences between Nehru and the princes. He disliked their lifestyle and mannerisms. The feeling was mutual; the princes disliked Nehru just as much. Had Nehru remained in charge of the merger of the princely states, the political map of India would have been dramatically different today. Patel, on the other hand, was admired across the board. In a manner of speaking, the style in which he achieved the task of merging the princely states proves that he was an imaginative and masterly statesman. Without Sardar Patel, there would have been no united India.

UNITED WE STAND

For the Congress, independence was the prime agenda. The question of princely states would arise only after Independence. There were more than 500 princely states all over India and the British were contemplating a federation of states, a united states of India. The British asserted that the princes would get to choose whether to accede to either dominion orremain independent. Jinnah was opposed to the idea of accession and announced that he would guarantee the independence of the states in Pakistan. Between the Congress and the British hung the princely states.

While most princely states contemplated a merger, the rulers of Orissa states rejected the idea and went on to form the Eastern States Union under the leadership of Maharaja Rajendra Narayan. They discussed the creation of a separate Eastern States Union for the Orissa Garjats—the princely states in the Orissa Tributary States and Chhattisgarh States Agency, which would, theoretically, be structured like the Eastern States Agency of 1933, which the British had formed by unifying the Chhattisgarh and Orissa States Agencies. The goal was to establish a unit large enough to exist as a state within the Indian dominion as well as share the cost of maintenance of an adequate security and military force to preserve law and order.

Out of the 40 states in the proposed Eastern States Union, 34 were Odia-speaking—the princely states of Sakti, Sarangarh, Raigarh, Udaypur, Jashpur and Surguja had a sizeable Odia population. Although Bindra-Nawagarh, Phuljhar and Deori had a high percentage of Laria speakers, the difference between Koshali and Odia, like Irish and English, is greater than it is between Odia and Laria. The region, which comprised of the Eastern States Union, was rich in minerals, precious stones, forest cover and water resources. Linguistically, economically and administratively the idea of the Union had merit.

A number of similar unions had already been formed: for instance, the Patiala and East Punjab States Union (PEPSU) went on to become a state of India, bringing together eight princely states; Matsya was the merger of four erstwhile princely states of Alwar, Bharatpur, Dholpur and Karauli; Saurashtra State, originally named the United State of Kathiawar, merged nearly 200 large and small princely states of colonial Baroda, Western India and Gujarat States Agency.

Lord Mountbatten, Mahatma Gandhi and Sitaramaya, president of All-India Garjat Praja Sammilani were not averse to the union. The Congress, however, opposed the Eastern States Union and intensified its campaign against it by branding it as a sort of 'rulers' trade union'. They argued that it was not sustainable because there was no linguistic unity among the states. Two major states—Mayurbhanj and Bastar—had opted out of the Union. The Congress pushed for a unified Orissa state, with the rulers merging their territories.

Other than merger or formation of a union, some princely states like the states of Hyderabad, Mysore, Kashmir and Travancore-Cochin had chosen to remain as independent territories on the map of India within the constitutional framework. The rulers of these territories acted as governors or heads of state.

As the movement for the Eastern States Union gathered momentum, unrest started erupting in some states like Nilgiri, Talcher and Dhenkanal. The Raja of Nilgiri had been deposed following a violent uprising[56], and a parallel government by the Praja Mandal was running the state. Faced with a law and

---

[56]The 1938 Praja Mandal movement in Nilgiri is a watershed moment in Orissa's history.

order problem, the dominion government at the centre was forced to pass an Extraterritorial Jurisdiction Act for the first time in the country and take over Nilgiri in November 1946. This event not only sent a grim message to the Garjats, but also accelerated the process and pace of merger. The message was clear; the provincial people's governments were hostile to the princes.

Facing a situation of insecurity and continuous disturbances of public order, the rulers of the states of the former Eastern States Agency formally founded the Eastern States Union in the Raj Kumar College building in Raipur. The Eastern States Union started functioning from 1 August 1947, just 14 days before India's independence.

MEDIATIONS FOR MERGER

The Congress wanted the princes to help in forming the Indian Union and leave sovereignty to their people. With this agenda, Patel and Mahatab soon began negotiations with the Eastern States. Menon had concluded that the only solution to a unified Orissa was to merge them all, to save the region from being swallowed up by Hyderabad, Chhattisgarh and the Central Provinces. The Raja of Kharsawan was hesitant to merge with Orissa, but after Patel explained to him that it was an interim arrangement and the final decision would be taken after consultation with the people, he agreed. Patel then also managed to convince the states of Athgarh, Baramba, Daspala, Hindol, Khandpara, Nilgiri, Talcher, Narsinghpur, Pal Lahara, Rairakhol and Ranpur.

The rulers of Bamra, Baudh, Dhenkanal, Gangpur, Kalahandi, Keonjhar, Mayurbhanj, Nayagarh, Patna, Seraikela and Sonepur were next in line. Patel, in discussion with the Orissa states had explained that he was there not as a member of the old paramountcy but as family.[57] Had they listened to his advice, they could have saved themselves from being uprooted by the people. The Maharaja of Mayurbhanj had already formed a popular government, establishing himself as the constitutional head. He could not commit anything before consulting the Cabinet. Patna, leading the rulers, opposed an outright merger. Instead, the Maharaja had an alternative view of two Orissa states: one, Seraikela-Kharsawan with Orissa Province and the other, the Garjats of Orissa with Bastar, Deobhog, Phuljhar, Sakti and Sarangarh, which would anyway merge into one in the foreseeable future when the decision to carve out the boundaries of provinces on linguistic lines was implemented. This alternative of two Orissa states would have eventually paved the path for a greater Orissa. It was not to be.

When the rulers met again, Patel reminded them of his earlier announcement wherein he had 'expressed the hope that the Indian states would bear in mind that the alternative to cooperation in the general interest was anarchy and chaos, which would overwhelm great and small in common ruin.'[58] The merger would save them from the fury of their subjects, who had been newly awakened to a consciousness of their rights. Patna sought a little more time as some of the rulers were members of the Eastern States Union.

During the deliberations with Rajendra Narayan, Patel almost lost his patience. If the department of states failed to achieve a merger in Orissa and Chhattisgarh, their first

---

[57]Basu, Narayani, *V.P. Menon: The Unsung Architect of Modern India,* S&S India, 2020.

[58]Ministry of States, 'Press Statement by Sardar Vallabhbhai Patel on 4th July, 1947', *White Paper on Indian States,* Ministry of States, Government of India, 1950, p. 34.

sincere attempt, the ripple effects would be felt across the remaining princely states and the integration of Indian states would be much harder to achieve. Sensing that the maharajas were stalling the negotiations to arrive at a better deal, Menon announced that he would send for the reserve police force and occupy the states to maintain law and order and that the offer to the maharajas would then be 'off the table, after which neither him nor Patel could answer for the consequences'.[59]

Although, Patna had worked against the merger, Rajendra Narayan now realized the futility of resistance. Patel and Menon had given their final offers. The Maharaja personally met Mahatma Gandhi on 3 December 1947 to seek his advice. Although, the outcome of that meeting is unknown, the wise ruler realized that the writing was on the wall. The Eastern States Union had proved to be an administrative failure. Many of its member states had acceded to the Union and there was intense Praja Mandal movement agitations in Hindol, Nilgiri, Dhenkanal and Talcher in December 1947.

FIRST TO MERGE

The Maharaja addressed his fellow rulers at this political juncture, which not only reveals the psychological pressure under which the rajas of Orissa were operating, but also provides a fairly clear idea of the impulse underlying Rajendra Narayan's first signature on the historic document of the merger:

> We may eventually be confronted with an impasse, which will compel us to take up arms against our own people. Speaking for myself, it would cause me deep anguish to be

[59]Basu, Narayani, *V.P. Menon: The Unsung Architect of Modern India,* S&S India, 2020.

> driven into any circumstances to fight my own people for whose welfare I have devoted most of my life and energy. I realize that we are at crossroads. If we try to resist the historical forces, we are doomed. The wave of democracy is rolling down on us. Either we step aside and let it roll on, or we stand in its way and get floundered. We cannot trick history and seek compromises and adjustments with the will of the people.
>
> But I believe it is better to shock with truth than soothe with a lie. It is no use shutting our eyes like an ostrich and believing that nobody sees us if we see nobody. We have to face the facts. I feel that it is a tragedy that our minds are so preoccupied with questions of paramountcy, honours and ceremonials, protections and safeguards that we have completely lost sight of one essential fact, i.e. is it in keeping with our ideals of Indian kingship that we should fight our own people and oppose their wishes in regard to the type of government they want for themselves? Maybe, they are wrong, but does it justify us to turn them into our enemies and become objects of their hatred? I won't like to wait till I am actually told to go by my own people. It would be a graceless exit and quite out of tune with our traditions and honour and self-respect.[60]

Patel and Menon were scheduled to leave on the morning of 15 December 1947. While boarding the plane for the airport, they received a telephone call from Patna to wait a little longer. Patel gave the Maharaja one hour's time to decide. After carefully going through each term in the Instrument of Accession, it was Patna who first signed the agreement. Others followed.

---

[60]Ministry of States, *White Paper on Indian States,* Government of India Press, Delhi, 1950.

Only Mayurbhanj remained. A year later, Mayurbhanj merged with Orissa. After the signing of the document, a privy purse was conceded to the rulers as a quid pro quo—they had not asked for it.

The Centre carefully and dextrously carried through with the merger plan. 'A former official of the political department,' Patel recounted, 'had warned me not to deal with Orissa first, as the rulers were supposed to be intractable.'[61] However, Patel decided to start with Orissa and Chhattisgarh because of the rising insurgency in Hyderabad. He used all means of persuasion and coercion to make the rajas see the 'sense'. While admitting that Patna was free from unrest, Patel said, 'I told the Maharaja it would not be long before the agitation spread to his state.' To Kalahandi's similar reply, he had warned, 'I'll send in communists to your state.'

The Maharaja signed the merger agreement and returned to Balangir. It was time to hand over the charge of the state to the administrator, Prafulla Chandra Tripathy. The royal treasury had around ₹52 lakh. While his counterparts drained the treasury dry, the Maharaja refunded the treasury with ₹6 lakh that were borrowed towards the marriage of his daughter, and passed on the treasury intact. His officers advised him to drain the treasury to the last coin like the other rulers of the Garjats. To this, he replied, 'I was born the second son of my father. I was not the first born. I was made a ruler. I have no right over the money of the people. It belongs to them.'[62]

---

[61]Menon, V.P., *The Story of the Integration of the Indian States*, Macmillan, New York, 1956.

[62]As told to Pabitra Mohan Nayak in a personal interview.

A day after the Maharaja signed away his state, he called a meeting of the officers and told them to show the same cooperation to the next administration and left for a farewell meeting at Rajendra Park. Thousands had poured from different corners of the state to attend the meeting and hear their dear, departing Maharaja. Rajendra Narayan alighted from the car, his lips lit up with a habitual smile. He looked as cheerful as when he was the sovereign ruler of the state. The Maharaja then left for Lucknow where he had decided to stay for the rest of his life, as his wife's, Maharani Kailash Kumari, sister lived there, and they wanted to remain close to her family. The Maharaja moved from his palace to a small house on a small plot of land at 30, Sarojini Naidu Marg.

Out of the remaining states in the region, Changbhakar, Kodia, Surguja, Jashpur, Udaipur, Raigarh, Sarangarh, Kawardha, Khairagarh, Nandgaon and Kanker became part of Madhya Pradesh.[63] Kharsawan and Seraikela joined Bihar in May 1948.

WORST FEARS COME TRUE

Back home at Balangir, life became hell after the merger. Thread, cloth, sugar and kerosene became scarce. The poor could not get rice at fair price. The villagers could not collect fuel from the forest. The police unleashed a reign of terror. Life had suddenly changed. Sudarshan Nayak, a leader of the people, became a strong critic of the Congress. There was firing at Kharsawan, Mayurbhanj and Bamanda. People felt their life and property were not safe under the new Congress government. They remembered their Maharaja all the more poignantly.

[63]Since 2000, most of the areas of the former princely states in eastern Madhya Pradesh belong to the state of Chhattisgarh.

An emissary representing the citizens of Balangir was sent to Lucknow to bring back the Maharaja. 'You've handed over the state to the government,' said the emissary, 'now you must bring the state to the people.'[64]

The Maharaja replied, 'The people have to fight for their right in a democracy. I have decided to go to the Himalayas and live the rest of my life in solitude. The Maharani will look after the education of my children here in Lucknow. This is my plan. The people of Patna should not drag me back.'[65]

But the emissary could not be put off so easily. He had been instructed to bring the Maharaja back with him. He threatened to resort to a hunger strike till the Maharaja said yes. On the day of Vijaya Dasami in 1948, the Maharaja returned to Balangir after offering worship at the temple of Goddess Vindhyavasini. This time not as Maharaja, but as a common man, dressed in a dhoti and kurta. He had put away his royal robe. The people, who had gathered in thousands in front of the Sailashree Palace, weighed him down with flowers, welcoming him. Upon his return, the Maharaja saw that his worst apprehensions had come true. He also assessed the political situation.

After Independence, Mahatma Gandhi was in favour of disbanding the Congress party. He believed that the party's objective, which was an independent Indian state, had been accomplished. Obviously, the political party did not disband. It was believed among those opposed to his views that they must make up for the losses India had sustained as a result of British rule, and preferably through the party that brought India freedom and them power. The National Congress had

---

[64]As recalled by A.U. Singh Deo.

[65]Excerpts from private letters and correspondences remaining with the Singh Deo family.

become a symbol of national sacrifice and pride.

The Congress party was evolving from its original philosophy and Gandhian ethics soon after Independence. There was no opposition or rival. After the merger of the princely states into the Indian Union, Patel had apparently declared that the rajas and nawabs, who had joined politics, would have to forfeit their privy purse. The princes were thus dependent on the Congress for the continuation of the privy purse—which although constitutionally guaranteed, could be reduced or eliminated, or even abolished as done by Indira Gandhi later in the 1970s—given the overwhelming legislative majority of the Congress. In fact, when the maharajas of Jodhpur and Baroda tried to form a rulers' union in 1951 against the merger of the princely states, the government deposed the Maharaja of Baroda of his title and purse.

Rajendra Narayan believed that the Congress, which had brought freedom, should not crush it. He also knew that a party, howsoever well-intentioned, tends to become dictatorial in the absence of a rival to question its policies. In his view, a strong opposition was necessary for the successful working of democracy.

It was against this backdrop that Rajendra Narayan decided to form an opposition that would effectively challenge the supremacy of the Congress in the state legislature. He therefore formed a new party called the Koshal Utkal Praja Parishad on the premises of Patna House at Sambalpur. Later, in a conference at Rajgangpur, the Koshal Utkal Praja Parishad was rechristened as the GP and reorganized into a full-fledged state-based political party with a definite objective, a definite principle and a definite ideal.

The Orissa government, headed by Dr Harekrushna Mahatab as CM, understood that the rise of a formidable opposition was underway and began preparing a counter propaganda. The Congress countered the rise of the Parishad by arguing that Rajendra Narayan was trying to revive the rule of the fourteenth century Patna Chauhans. Undeterred, Rajendra Narayan and the party worked as the chief opposition in the state legislature from 1952 to 1961, till it merged with the Swatantra Party after the parliamentary election of 1962.

Before we start discussing about the political developments, some context on the Odia districts outside of the erstwhile state is necessary.

4

The Lost Districts

For many people, Orissa is just a geographic name—a state of India with a vague history of its own, abounding in hills and forests and subject to constant famine and flood. Few outside the state know that the history of Odisha dates back to the ancient kingdom of Kalinga—invaded by the Mauryan emperor Ashoka in 261 BCE that resulted in the Kalinga War—located between the Mahanadi and Godavari rivers, or that the boundaries of this powerful kingdom coincide with the borders of modern-day Odisha. Kalinga's maritime prowess had enabled its people to settle in far off lands such as Java, Borneo and Sumatra. The impact on the ancient economy was such that even today Indians are known in these regions as Kling.[66]

Sambalpur and the adjacent Odia-speaking feudatory states were included in the Central Provinces in 1862 for administrative convenience while Orissa was an administrative division of the Bengal Presidency before it became a

[66]Indians are called Kling in Java, Borneo and Sumatra because they traded with Kalinga in ancient times. There was no India then.

sub-province of Bihar in 1874. Later in the same year, the British proposed to constitute Assam and Orissa as separate provinces. In 1883, the Garjats with Singbhum and other Chhattisgarh states were brought under South-Western Frontier Agency (SWF) with Ranchi as its headquarters. The government, however, found this region difficult to administer due to the language barrier. For instance, the Hindi-speaking officers of the Central Provinces were reluctant to be transferred to Sambalpur, while the Odia-speaking officers would similarly refuse a transfer to Hindi-speaking areas.

By 1903 therefore, Sir H.H. Risley, home secretary to the Government of India, wrote to the respective governments of Bengal, Madras, Central Provinces and Berar[67] to unite the entire Odia-speaking tracts, both hill and plains, under one administration in order to enable a single government to deal with Odia problems and to relieve other governments 'of a troublesome excrescence upon their administrative system'. Such a scheme, he hoped, 'would solve the question of language once for all'.[68]

BIRTH OF ORISSA PROVINCE

In 1905, with the partition of Bengal, Sambalpur district—except Phujhar, Chandrapur and Borasambar—Padampur, Patna, Sonepur, Bamra, Rairakhol, Bonai and Gangpur were retransferred to the Orissa division of Bengal, while Raigarh, Sarangarh, Sakti, Chandrapur, Padampur, Phuljhar and Khariar

[67]Berar was a province in British India, corresponding to present-day Vidarbha in the eastern region of Maharashtra, then administered by the British. Although, the Nizam of Hyderabad had permanently leased Berar to the British in 1902, the Nizam retained formal sovereignty over this region.

[68]Devi, Bandita, *Some Aspects of British Administration in Orissa, 1912-1936,* Academic Foundation, 1922.

were left under Chhatisgarh division of the Central Provinces. Odia was declared as the official language in Sambalpur and the adjacent feudatory states. However, this did not entirely resolve the issue. There were still Odia-speaking people in Madras Presidency who demanded amalgamation with Orissa. To look into the redistribution of territories, the government therefore constituted the Phillip–Duff Committee in 1924 that included two civilians, one from Bihar-Orissa and the other from Madras. The committee recommended that the Odia-speaking estates left within the administrative control of other provinces must be merged with Orissa. The report provoked a protest from the Madras government that refused to be guided by its recommendations, compelling the government to refer the matter to the Simon Commission[69] that was visiting India in 1928.

Unable to reach consensus or conclusion, the Government of India, in September 1931, constituted the Orissa Boundary Committee, headed by Samuel O'Donnell, to look into setting up a separate administration of the Odia-speaking people. However, the O'Donnell-headed committee's recommendations for the new province of Orissa excluded key areas like Singhbhum, Midnapore and some areas in the Central Provinces and in Ganjam from the proposed boundary line.

Disappointed, the Odia people protested for the inclusion of areas like Icchapore, Manjusa, Buddarsingh, Jalantar and Tarala of Ganjam, Singhbhum of Chotanagpur, Phuljhar and other Odia-speaking tracts of Raipur district and areas from Midnapore.

Meanwhile, in December 1932, the Government of India declared that a separate province of Orissa would be formed. However, the boundaries of the proposed Orissa Province, as

---

[69]Also known as the Indian Statutory Commission.

published in March 1933, reduced the total area to come under Orissa Province with the exclusion of Vizagapatam Agency, Jalantar Malia and Paralakhemundi.

It was declared that the new Orissa Province would be headed by a governor and would consist of the districts of Cuttack, Puri, Balasore, Angul and Sambalpur. From the Central Provinces, seven villages and the estates of Khariar and Padampur were restored to new Orissa Province. From the Madras Presidency, certain areas of the Ganjam Kills Tract Agency and some taluks of Ganjam district—north of the line joining Sonepur and Purusottampur via Surla Salt Factory—were included.

The government had, unfortunately, followed the O'Donnell Committee Report to the detriment of Orissa's interests. On 1 April 1936, Orissa was declared a separate province with Cuttack as the provincial capital and Puri as the summer headquarters. But it was a province splintered from its past.

HISTORICAL ONENESS

Large areas of land and people, linguistically, racially and culturally connected with Orissa remained out of its officially demarcated boundary. Many of the Odia-speaking tracts remained tagged to neighbouring provinces of Madras, Bihar, Bengal and the Central Provinces. For instance, in the Mahasamund tehsil of Raipur (present-day Chhattisgarh), which included Phuljhar, Bindra-Nawagarh, Bhatgan, Narra and Deori, Odia-speakers outnumbered Chhattisgarhi or Laria-speakers; Raigarh, which is contiguous to Sundargarh and Sambalpur districts of Orissa, comprised the ex-princely states of Raigarh, Bargarh, Sarangarh, Sakti and Chandrapur, and constituted the Athargarh confederacy of Patna-Sambalpur estate on the eve of British occupation of Orissa in 1803.

On the other hand, Bastar with 13,000 sq. miles, surrounded by Kanker, Mahasamund tehsil of Raipur and Durg districts—Chandrapur, Andhra and Koraput—was considered as a no man's land in which no language or race was expected to be in absolute majority. Bastar had once acknowledged the suzerainty of Sambalpur under Balaram Dev, while Bastar and Kanker had intermarriages within Sambalpur and Sonepur families. It is economically, racially, culturally, ethnically and even climatically connected with West Orissa. While Jagdalpur, barely five miles east of Bastar, lies 180 miles from Raipur, the capital city of Chattisgarh state today, it is only 13 miles from the Orissa border. Demonstrating linguistic unity, even the treaty between Jeypore and Bastar ceding Kotpad Paragana[70] was drawn in Odia in 1778. The Nagpur Resolution of the Congress in 1921, too, had favoured the amalgamation of Bastar with Orissa.

The Singhbhum district of modern-day Jharkhand has Manbhum[71] and Ranchi in the north, Midnapore (West Bengal) in the east, Keonjhar and Mayurbhanj in the south and Sundergarh (Orissa) to the west. The paraganas[72] of Barabhum and Patkum in South Manbhum, forming the northern boundary, are indisputably Odia areas. The zamindar of Barabhum (present-day Jharkhand) was a dependent chief under Mayurbhanj. Midnapore was considered a part of Orissa in the Diwani grant[73] to the East India Company in 1765, by

[70]The Kotpad Pargana consisting of the five forts of Kotpad, Churchund, Padaguda, Umerkote and Paigarh, originally formed a part of the native state of Bastar, which was then under the sovereignty of the Marathas of Nagpur.

[71]Present-day Purulia district of West Bengal.

[72]Paraganas is an old Indian term for administrative units.

[73]Diwani grant were the rights granted to British East India Company to collect revenue and decide on civil cases.

the emperor of Delhi. Thus, Singhbhum stands within the natural boundary of Orissa and includes Dhalbhum (present-day Jharkhand), that formed part of Utkal Desh.

Even according to the 1951 census, Dhalbhum had three linguistic zones: northern zone with Hindi, middle zone with Bengali and southern zone with Odia predominance. Jamshedpur excluded, Dhalbhum had 108,000 Odia-speaking, 104,000 Bengali-speaking, 46,000 Hindi-speaking and 97,000 Santali-speaking population.[74] A scientific, philological study of most of the tribal dialects too reveals their resemblance with Odia, whether it is Panchpargania or Kurmali or Bathudi. [75]On ethnic considerations too, the language of the aborigines of Singhbhum belongs to the Munda branch of the Austro-Asiatic family, whereas the Oraons of Ranchi speak a Dravidian language. Author B.C. Mazumdar in his book, *Aborigines of the Highlands of Central India*, states that the Savaras tribe are linked with the Kols (Hos), and Savaras as a race are found only in Orissa.

Thus Orissa, not Bihar, is the natural homeland of the Hos in particular and other aborigines in general. There is a minister of tribal welfare in Orissa, not in Bihar. Besides, as early as 1930, the noted anthropologist S.C. Ray had suggested to the Bihar and Orissa commissioner that the integration of not only the district of Singhbhum but entire Chota Nagpur with Orissa was necessary to ensure the well-being of the tribals.[76]

In addition to Singhbhum, Orissa also claimed southwest Midnapore, which includes Jhargram, Contai, Kharagpur,

---

[74]Gopalaswami, R.A., *Census of India, 1951*, Vol. I, https://bit.ly/3w7Xug4. Accessed on 9 May 2022.

[75]Ahmed, M., *Census of India, 1951*, Vol. XI, Orissa, Section II, https://bit.ly/3ylS3wP. Accessed on 9 May 2022.

[76]Dasgupta, Sangeeta, 'The journey of an anthropologist in Chhotanagpur', The Indian Economic and Social History Review, 1 April 2004, *Sage Journals*.

Dantan, Nandigram and Panskura. Midnapore, acquired by the British in 1760, was in Orissa division from 1829 to 1854 after which it was transferred to the Burdwan[77] division.

Rajendra Narayan believed that the people of these lands belonged to Orissa, linguistically, racially and culturally. They had been wronged and separated from their land when the boundaries of the Orissa Province were redesigned. He vowed to work for the unification of these territories with Orissa, especially after he had assumed the office of president of Utkal Sammilani—a body founded by the social reformer Madhusudan Das in 1903 with the sole objective of the reunification of Odia-speaking tracts in the neighbouring provinces in the north, south and west.

The former Maharaja, therefore, collected and compiled all the facts and figures, demonstrating the historical unity of these territories with Orissa and sent a memorandam on 28 May 1954 to the union government. However, of all demands, his birthplace, Seraikela and Kharsawan—no longer a part of Orissa—were as much close to his heart as the sentiments of the people of Orissa because these were politically, historically, linguistically and culturally a part of Orissa.

ORISSA'S OWN

In peace and prosperity, war and adventure, calamity and catastrophe, customs and traditions, rites and rituals, art and literature, the people of the large stretch of land between the Rusikulya and Subarnarekha rivers follow the same rhythms of life as those of Mayurbhanj, Bonai, Keonjhar, etc. of Orissa. There is even an unmistakable similarity in the way they name their houses and address their kin.

---

[77]Present-day Bardhaman, West Bengal.

That Seraikela was once a part of Orissa, has been established by history and historians. It finds mention even in the puranas. The 'Visnukhanda' of Skanda Purana places Seraikela in Odra Desa or Utkala Desa. So do ancient historians like General Douglas Hamilton, William Wilson Hunter and Sterling as well as modern historians like M.M. Chakravarti, F.E. Pargiter and R.D. Banerjee.

Irish indologist V.A. Smith observed that coins made from Singhbhum copper mines were issued by the rulers of Kalinga. Yet it was an irony of history that Seraikela and Kharsawan, which were part of the SWF along the Sambalpur states till 1854, were left under the administration of the commissioner of Chota Nagpur, with which they were neither historically, culturally nor linguistically linked. In 1915, they represented for transfer to the Sambalpur political agent. They agitated before the Butler Committee of 1916 and Sir Arthur Lothien Committee of 1931. Sir Arthur was of the view that the injustice done to Seraikela had to be reverted.

Celebrated linguist Sir George Grierson in *Linguistic Survey of India*[78] states that 'Singhbhum-Seraikela-Kharsawan was the proper home of Odia language and the Biharis in Singhbhum were "strangers in a strange land"'.[79] The 1931 census report maintains that while the Odia and Bengali speakers in Sareikela and Kharsawan numbered 51,206 and 45,264, respectively, out of a total population of 196,622, the Hindi Speakers were only 10,226.[80] As the deputy commissioner in Singbhum, B.C. Sen was aware of this historical fact and

[78]The *Linguistic Survey of India* was a comprehensive survey of the languages of British India conducted between 1894 and 1928 that describes 364 languages and dialects. The project was conducted under the direction of George A. Grierson, an official of the ICS.

[79]*Liguistic Survey of India,* Vol. 5, Pt. 2, Government Printing, Calcutta, p. 371.

[80]Hutton, H.J., *Census Of India 1931*, Vol. I.

expressed surprise on 26 January 1944 as to why Hindi and Bengali, and not Odia, continued as the medium used at court and school, respectively.

On 15 December 1947, when the rajas of Seraikela[81] and Kharsawan signed the Instrument of Accession, along with the 24 Garjats to merge with Orissa, the Government of India merged Seraikela and Kharsawan into one district with headquarters at Seraikela and appointed an administrator. A year later, the Orissa government assumed the administration of these states on behalf of the Indian dominion, but that was not to be for long.

BROKEN LIMBS OF ORISSA

In 1948, around the same time when Orissa took charge of its territories, the Bihar government swung into action and passed the Seraikela and Kharsawan Administration Order of 1948, effectively establishing claim and control over the administration of the two territories. It is also alleged that some elements acting under the endorsement of the Bihar province mobilized the tribals of Kharsawan in favour of Bihar, leading to a huge gathering of armed tribals in the mango groves on the outskirts of Kharsawan. The agitating tribals demanded to know from the Raja why he had signed the merger agreement without seeking their consent.

In Seraikela, too, there was an equally huge gathering of adivasis from Jamshedpur and Chainbasa. But when the Seraikela Raja explained to them the extenuating circumstances in which he had to sign the agreement, they returned

[81]Raja Aditya Pratap Singh Deo, the last ruler of Seraikela and Rajendra Narayan Singh Deo's biological father, signed the merger agreement for Seraikela, acceding to the Indian Union on 18 May 1947.

convinced. The same thing could have happened at Kharsawan, but for the administrator who made the mistake of using excessive force. Sensing that the demonstration may get out of hand, the administrator, unfortunately, decided to open fire on the rebels.

This incident tilted the case in Bihar's favour. Kharsawan went the Bihar way, but Seraikela remained with Orissa. Recalling Kharsawan's reluctance to sign the merger agreement, Menon writes in his book, *The Story of the Integration of the Indian States*, that the Raja of Kharsawan was initially in favour of a merger with Bihar as it was surrounded on all sides by Singhbhum. 'I persuaded him to sign the merger agreement. Later the merger issue could be decided through plebiscite. The Raja agreed.' No sooner was the agreement sealed that the question of plebiscite was forgotten. Even the merger with Orissa, which was a precondition to signing the Instrument of Accession, was neither fulfilled nor challenged.

There was now an unseemly controversy between Bihar and Orissa. The rajas of Seraikela and Kharsawan had acceded on the condition that they would merge with Orissa, but later merged into Bihar. In view of this, the Government of India issued a notification for appointment of a one-man tribunal with Justice Bavdekar of the Bombay High Court. The tribunal was to adjudicate upon the rival claims of Bihar and Orissa under specific terms of reference: the wishes of the people of the state, historical, economic, linguistic and cultural affinity and administrative convenience. However, before the committee could examine the issue and make its recommendations, the Government of India jumped the gun.

It asked the tribunal to cease work and in a clear breach of trust and treaty with Seraikela and Kharsawan and the people of Orissa, it authorized the delivery of Seraikela-Kharsawan to Bihar for administrative convenience. It claimed that these areas were an island territory and had no clear geographical contiguity with Orissa. Seraikela-Kharsawan was passed on to Bihar on 18 May 1948. The formal merger would happen later.

Three days later, noted lawyer, Maharaj Sri Nagendra Singh, on behalf of the Government of India, sought the willingness from Seraikela-Kharsawan for final integration with Bihar. Raja Aditya Pratap of Seraikela prayed that this could be done as an interim arrangement with his sovereignty over Seraikela state and its territorial integrity be left untouched till the Constitution of India was framed.[82] By that time, he expected that neighbouring Mayurbhanj would have merged with Orissa, paving the way for the amalgamation of Seraikela with Orissa. The Raja signed the agreement, and Bihar was jubilant.

Sri Krishna Sinha, CM of Bihar, after a victory celebration, made a public announcement on 5 June 1948: 'I assure the Odias of these states of Seraikela and Kharsawan that their language, culture and individual rights will be duly protected and safeguarded by my government.' It is another matter, however, that back in Ranchi, his government released a press note stating: 'The Governor of Bihar is pleased to declare that Hindi and Devanagari shall be the court language and script, respectively, in the areas comprised within the said states.'

Was the promise to protect the Odia identity forgotten? Rajendra Narayan, by then a political figure, sent a telegram to the Governor General against the promulgation of Hindi in courts. But to no avail. With the districts of Seraikela and Kharsawan taken away from Orissa and merged with Bihar, Rajendra Narayan felt as though Orissa had lost a limb.

---

[82]A.P. Singh Deo, 3 Landsdown Road, Calcutta, letter to Nagendra Singh, Tripura House, Calcutta, 23 May 1948.

STRUGGLE FOR REUNION

The CMs of Central Provinces, Bihar, Bengal and Orissa made a joint statement that they accepted the decision of the Government of India in regard to the distribution of former native states belonging to the Eastern States Agency and there was no controversy between them on that account. Also, they would not claim further additions of territories into their states. Dr Mahatab was then CM of Orissa. Between the lines, this meeting meant that these states had accepted the amalgamation of Seraikela-Kharsawan with Bihar.

Unlike these CMs, most people, including the Raja of Seraikela, who had signed over his erstwhile estate to Bihar, and even Rajendra Narayan perceived that the integration of Seraikela and Kharsawan into Bihar was in the nature of a stop gap arrangement. For instance, Patel's reply on 10 August 1948 to a supplementary question by a noted member of the Constituent Assembly in the proceedings was rather intriguing and open to interpretation. He said that nothing is permanent in this transitory world. The reply was as much diplomatic as it was philosophical to a purely political question.

In early 1949, as the date of formal merger with Bihar drew closer, Raja Aditya Pratap of Seraikela lodged a protest with the Government of India against the seemingly secret pact among the CMs to accept the two territories as part of Bihar. He also wrote to Sardar Patel stating that he had agreed to merge his state with Bihar as a temporary measure for administrative convenience, but given the merger of Mayurbhanj with Orissa, that condition no longer remained valid.[83] On 6 May 1949, he wrote to Menon that the remerger issue may be settled in accordance with the wishes of the people. Therefore, Seraikela-

[83]A.P. Singh Deo, DO Letter No. 15 to Sardar Patel, Ministry of States, Government of India, New Delhi, 1949.

Kharsawan should be, once again, merged with Orissa.

He also sent a representation to the Governor General and PM Nehru:

> The notification of merger (with Bihar) under Section 290 A of the Government of India Act comes to us all as a shock and it leads us to a conviction that it has been done in contravention of the letter and spirit both of the British Cabinet Plan and the agreement of the negotiating team of the Constituent Assembly and the Government of India. Further, it is a clear repudiation of the terms of the agreement on 15 December 1947 at Cuttack in the presence of Sardar Patel. The integration with Bihar cannot be complete and effective, and much less final even in terms of Section 290 A of the Act.
>
> The Government of India in their White Paper records the helpful attitude of the Indian princely states in surrendering their states and status. It assured us that no change in our agreement will be effected without our consent. Need I also state, all my brother princes of Orissa states have no less been distressed than myself regarding this as a tragedy of the first magnitude? Is it too much to claim that the terms of the agreement of integration be accepted or in the alternative the wishes of myself and my state subjects be consulted before the integration is finalized?[84]

The Government of India replied that the two states had been formally merged with Bihar permanently on 26 July 1949, the Governor General of India promulgated the states merger order that resulted in the formal merger of the former princely

[84]'State Of Seraikella vs Union Of India And Another', indiankanoon, https://bit.ly/3DJOjpC. Accessed on 6 April 2022.

states of Seraikela-Kharsawan into the province of Bihar.[85] Shortly thereafter, the Seraikela Raja then went to the Supreme Court,[86] where he questioned the constitutional propriety of tearing apart these Odia states and tagging them to Bihar with which they had nothing in common. The Raja contended that the province of Bihar had wrongfully and illegally taken over the administration of the state and passed the Seraikela and Kharsawan administration order.

The Court thus dismissed the Raja's petition. While Bihar and the Centre were parties to the case, the Orissa government was not. The Union Cabinet asserted that Seraikela had dug its own ditch by agreeing to merge with Bihar, and Orissa had nothing to do with it. The Raja realized then that it would not hurt the Congress government in Orissa to keep two influential Garjat states out, which would have naturally come under the influence of Rajendra Narayan, given that the people desired unity with Orissa. When the merger order was issued for instance, there was a tremendous popular agitation in Singhbhum, Seraikela and Kharsawan in favour of going with the state of Orissa. The fire had spread. The Bihar government did its best to suppress the agitation. The attitude of the Bihar government, however, was greatly resented by the top leaders of the country. Even Nehru was quoted saying, 'At the present moment of our history when some of the smaller states have been merged into a province, a neighbouring province has objected with such violence that one would think that two countries were on the verge of war.'[87]

---

[85]M.K. Vellodi, ICS, secretary to Government of India, Ministry of States, Letter No. D7143 P/49 to A.P. Singh Deo, 22 August 1949.

[86]'State Of Seraikella vs Union Of India And Another', indiankanoon, https://bit.ly/3DJOjpC. Accessed on 6 April 2022.

[87]*Parliamentary Debates, House of the People: Official Report,* Vol. 1, Parliament Secretariat, New Delhi, 1952, https://bit.ly/3x8lAcN. Accessed on 6 April 2022.

Rajendra Narayan noted that the day of the formal merger of Seraikela and Kharsawan with Bihar would remain a dark day in the annals of independent, democratic India, when the voice of the people was silenced by the Bihar government, through indiscriminate beating and a brutal assault on the citizens of Seraikela and Kharsawan in the open streets, in broad daylight.[88] The agitation for reunion gathered momentum. It even exceeded the intensity of the Praja Mandal movements during the freedom struggle.

When the crackdown by the authorities against this unrest was at its height, Raja Aditya Pratap requested the Centre to intervene. Sardar Patel, on the other hand, requested the Raja to meet with Dr Rajendra Prasad, then chairman of the Constituent Assembly, who was from Bihar. This seemed like a political move given that the interprovincial dispute was the sole jurisdiction of the home ministry and had nothing to do with the Constituent Assembly. Aditya Pratap, to honour the wishes of Sardar Patel, sought time for a meeting with Dr Prasad, which was not given. The Raja then wrote to convey his discontentment to M.K. Vellodi, ICS, and secretary to Government of India: 'If the Government of India goes back on the assurances and effects a breach themselves in our agreement, without consultation and without my assent, could it be too much to apprehend that my other conditions of the agreement may similarly be done away with without consultation and consent. It is this aspect of the question that has not only upset me but all the rulers of Orissa

---

[88]He noted this at the meeting of the princes at the Sailashree Palace in the aftermath of the firing incident. The meeting and remark were recalled by HH Raj Raj Singh Deo, his son, and is also mentioned in the private book published by them.

and Chhattisgarh who have signed similar agreements.'[89]

HOPE ON THE HORIZON

On 29 December 1953, the Government of India had constituted the States Reorganisation Commission (SRC) with the objective of reconstituting provinces on the basis of language and redrawing interprovincial boundaries. This rekindled the hopes of the people of Orissa, which had the unique distinction of being a province formed on the basis of language for the first time in the country. But without a true formation of Odia-speaking regions within the territory, it remained a fragmented state.

The hope for a complete Orissa was renewed when Rajendra Narayan was elected president of the Utkal Sammilani in the same year. Long memoirs were prepared for submission to the SRC. The need of the hour was a sustained effort by the ruling party and Opposition to achieve this objective. However, Rajendra Narayan faced an almost uphill task both within Orissa and in Delhi in the midst of a hostile Congress, who was in power at both levels of government.

Rajendra Narayan wrote to Dr Mahatab, who was, by then, a minster at the Centre, to influence the government of Orissa. However, Dr Mahatab responded, stating that the Orissa government needed no outside help to put forth its demand before the commission. In fact, the Orissa Pradesh Congress Committee (OPCC) had resolved that the government needed no cooperation from any non-official organization (the primary implication of the same being Utkal Sammilani) to face the SRC. This resolution was published in the mass circulated

[89]Kania, H.J., 'State Of Seraikella vs Union Of India And Another', 1951 AIR 253, https://bit.ly/3DJOjpC. Accessed on 6 April 2022.

and widely read Odia daily, *The Samaj,* of which Radhanath Rath, state minister of finance, was the editor.

Rajendra Narayan also raised the issue of Seraikela and Kharsawan in the Parliament whenever there was scope. On 7 July 1952, as an MP, he moved a resolution that Seraikela and Kharsawan be immediately restored to Orissa in accordance with the terms of the merger agreement. On 17 February 1954, during the Budget Session after the president's address, he gave a long, well-considered speech in which he raised the Seraikela-Kharsawan issue. While thanking the government for the constitution of SRC, he questioned the sincerity of its intention for states reorganization. He said:

> For centuries, Seraikela and Kharsawan have been known as the Orissa states. The people speak Odiya. They were grouped together in one administration with the other states in Orissa. But subsequently, there was a dispute between Orissa and Bihar and in deciding that dispute, all principles of democracy, which our leaders used to shout from house tops were thrown overboard and I am sorry to say that principles became the first victim to the whim of persons at the helm. An inconsistent policy was followed in regard to those states and an inconsistent decision arrived at.[90]

He also pointed out in the Lok Sabha that 'the merger agreement was a legal, constitutional, material and moral document. What happened to it? As the fundamental democratic principle of ascertaining the wishes of the people before the integration of the Indian states was completely ignored and denied, the Garjats of Orissa had sought formation of Eastern States Union.'

---

[90]*Parliamentary Debates, House of the People: Official Report*, Vol. 1, Parliament Secretariat, New Delhi, 1954.

Calling it 'a tragedy too deep for tears', he asserted that the government of Orissa, under the plea of seizing pistols, had seized pamphlets and leaflets, which they thought to be more explosive than arms and ammunitions. When the home minister alleged in response that those who did not allow meetings to be held and newspapers to be published in their states were now in Parliament stating that civil liberties are being destroyed, Rajendra Narayan asked,

> Are you going to justify measures of this kind by such arguments? Suppose there were badly administered states, are you going to compete with them? Will you detain people without trial, going against Article 9 of the Universal Declaration of Human Rights, simply because they alleged they were not consulted before their states were merged? What happened to the Cabinet Mission Plan of 16 May 1946? Where are the recommendations of the Atlee sub-committee of the Simon Commission now? Where have the canons of justice, equity and fair play gone?[91]

He asserted that the persistent agitation during the last five years in the face of inhuman repression is an epic story of heroic suffering and endurance.

He maintained that with this forced dismemberment, the seeds of disunity, however invisible, have been sown. The discontentment remained. The spark could not be put out by repression. Referring to the SRC, he said, 'Here is an opportunity for redressing the wrongs of the past and for creating the atmosphere necessary for harmonious development of the different races in the country bound together by ties of language and culture, each according to its needs and genius, with a common natural goal.' Raja Aditya Pratap also appealed

---

[91]Ibid.

to the SRC for an interim report so that the 'suspense holding the people may abate and the tension between the two states could cease'.

On 10 October 1955, the SRC report came out. It stated that as Singhbhum was not included in Orissa by the Orissa by the O'Donnell Committee, Seraikela-Kharsawan, which were a part of Singhbhum, could not go to Orissa. The commission report did not consider the fact that Seraikela and Kharsawan were already independent in 1931 when the committee was set up!

Nabakrushna Choudhuri, then Orissa CM, declared in the Assembly that the SRC report was more devastating than the Dalei Ghai flood[92] of 1955. This statement was printed in *The Samaj* and widely circulated among the people. The publication also carried an editorial titled, '*Sabas, Congress*! [Congrats, Congress!]' When a discussion was demanded on the floor of the Assembly, the Speaker refused the motion. Rajendra Narayan leading the Utkal Sammilani and Godabarish Mishra, president of the GP in a joint statement condemned the SRC report and appealed to all parties and the Orissa government to come under one umbrella and formulate a joint action plan above party lines.

On 16 January 1956, the SRC report was adopted by Parliament. The OPCC openly dissented and even passed a resolution expressing its inability to run the administration and the organization in the changed circumstances. Even while appealing to the people in and outside Orissa to resort to peaceful and constitutional means to fulfil their demands, the Congress, after carefully considering different issues deeply felt that by rejecting demands based on just, reasonable and

[92]In 1955–56, there was a major flood in which Dalei Ghai embankment (near Jagatsingpur) breached causing extensive damage in large areas in Mahanadi Delta.

irrefutable facts, the burden of injustice was being imposed on Orissa forever. The Congress protested against this injustice. Judging from the anxiety of the leaders of the country regarding the peaceful and satisfactory solution of the problems relating to states' reorganization, the committee strongly opined that it could be resolved only by considering the situation of the regions concerned from the point of justice and impartiality. It would be unjust if this principle was ignored by taking advantage of the comparatively weak and peace-loving provinces. The committee felt that there had been no clear principles adopted while deciding all the facts regarding Orissa. Therefore, after discussing every aspect of the issues and considering the principles adopted since the beginning and giving due importance to the prevailing popular opinion, the committee felt that it was its duty to lodge a protest in a disciplined and constitutional way while keeping its faith in peaceful and constitutional methods. The committee also felt that it was impossible for Congress members, who were entrusted with the different government responsibilities, to discharge them.[93]

Meanwhile, the ground situation at Orissa was beginning to get hostile. The border agitation became a spontaneous mass movement. The Secretariat had to be shut down. Offices were closed and trains and bus services were suspended. The agitation was widespread, from Cuttack in the east to Kalahandi in the west and Koraput in the south to Keonjhar in the north.

The police were eventually forced to open fire on the protesters and curfew was imposed on many areas of the state. Section 144 was also imposed to prevent large gatherings. Popular Odia leaders and intellectuals such as Pt Godabarish Mishra, Surendra Mohanty, Sarangadhar Das and Rajendra

---

[93]Editorial, *The Prajatantra*, 19 January 1956.

His Highness Maharaja Rajendra Narayan Singh Deo of Patna state

The Maharaja and Her Highness Maharani Kailash Kumari Devi of Patna

Coronation of the Maharaja in 1924

Young Rajendra Narayan Singh Deo as Yuvraj of Patna

Yuvraj Rajendra Narayan Singh Deo at his sacred thread ceremony, flanked by his adoptive father, His Highness Maharaja Prithviraj Singh Deo, and his biological father, Raja Aditya Pratap Singh Deo of Seraikela

The Maharaja (second from left), with his siblings Rajkumari Hem Prabha Devi, Pattayet Bhoopendra Narayan Singh Deo, Tikayat Nripendra Narayan Singh Deo and Rajkumari Ratna Prabha Devi

(Standing from left) Rajkumar Shuvendra Narayan Singh Deo, Tikayet Nripendra Narayan Singh Deo, Raja Jagannath Rajmani Raj Deo, the Maharaja, Pattayet Bhoopendra Narayan Singh Deo and Yuvraj Shata Bhanu Singh Deo

(Sitting from left) Tikayetrani Kusum Manjari Devi carrying infant Lal Saheb Juga Bhanu Singh Deo, Rani Padmini Kumari Devi, Maharani Kailash Kumari Devi

(Seated on the floor from left) Rajkumari Manjushree Devi, Maharajkumari Braj Shree Devi, Lal Saheb Suro Bhanu Singh Deo, Yuvraj Raj Raj Singh Deo, Rajkumari Jayshree Devi and Maharajkumari Raj Shree Devi

(Left to right) Rajkumari Hem Prava Devi, Tikayet Nripendra Narain Singh Deo, Rajkumari Mani Prabha Devi, the Maharaja (standing) and Rajkumari Ratna Prava Devi

(Left to right) Rajkumari Manjushree Devi, Maharajkumari Rajshree Devi, Lal Saheb Juga Bhanu Singh Deo (infant), Yuvraj Shata Bhanu Singh Deo, Yuvraj Raj Raj Singh Deo.

(Sitting from left) Rajkumari Jayshree Devi, Maharajkumari Braj Shree Devi and Lal Saheb Suro Bhanu Singh Deo

The Maharaja's elder son, Maharaja Raj Raj Singh Deo, and Maharani Premlata Kumari Devi of Patna, Balangir

The Maharaja's younger son, Maharajkumar Ananga Uday Singh Deo, and Rani Vijay Lakshmi Singh Deo

The Maharaja's eldest daughter, Rani Saheba Raj Shree Devi, and Raja Prithvirajsinjhi of Sayla

The Maharaja's second daughter, Rani Braj Shree Devi, with Raja Mahendra Ripudaman Singh of Bhadawar

The Maharaja's third daughter, Rani Roop Shri Devi, with Zamindar Saheb Ran Vijay Shahi of Dumaria, Bihar

The Maharaja's fourth daughter, Rani Krishna Kumari Singh, with Captain Kunwar Baldev Singh of Jalalpur-Aligarh

Maharaja Raj Raj Singh Deo's elder son, Maharaja Kanak Vardhan Singh Deo, and Maharani Sangeeta Singh Deo of Balangir, Patna

Maharaja Raj Raj Singh Deo's younger son, Maharajkumar Sri Vardhan Singh Deo, and Rani Prakriti Kumari Devi

Daughter of Maharaja Raj Raj Singh Deo, Thakurani Mitra Binda Kumari, and Colonel Yudhisthir Panwar SM, VSM of the 3rd Battalion, Parachute Regiment

Maharaja Raj Raj Singh Deo's another daughter, Rani Satya Rajeshwari Singh, with Kunwar Sanjay Singh Badnor

Maharajkumar Anang Uday Singh Deo's eldest son, Rajkumar Kalikesh Narayan Singh Deo, and Rani Meghna Singh Deo

Maharajkumar Anang Uday Singh Deo's second son, Rajkumar Manmath Vijay Singh Deo, with Rani Deepshika Singh Deo

Maharajkumar Anang Uday Singh Deo's youngest son, Arkesh Narayan Singh Deo, with Rani Adrija Manjari Singh Deo

(Left to right) The Maharaja's grandsons, Rajkumar Arkesh Narayan Singh Deo, Rajkumar Manmath Vijay Singh Deo and Rajkumar Kalikesh Narayan Singh Deo

(Left to right) Rani Deepshikha Singh Deo, Maharajkumar Anang Uday Singh Deo, Rajkumar Arkesh Narayan Singh Deo, Rajkumar Kalikesh Narayan Singh Deo, Rajkumar Manmath Vijay Singh Deo, Rani Adrija Manjari Singh Deo (seated), Rani Vijay Lakshmi Devi and Rani Meghna Singh Deo

Adopted son of Maharaja Rajendra Narayan Singh Deo, Dr Kumar Sridutt Baboo, and wife, Kumud

Former President of India, Dr Rajendra Prasad (centre), with The Maharaja (fourth from left)

Khan Abdul Ghaffar Khan (left) with the Maharaja, chief minister of Orissa

(Left to right) Then chief minister of Orissa, Harekrushna Mahatab, Finance Minister Maharaja Rajendra Narayan Singh Deo, Industries Minister Raja Bir Udit Pratap Shekhar Deo of Gangpur in the coalition cabinet of 1959–61

Prime Minister's XI vs. President's XI Cricket Match, 1953; the Maharaja (second from left) with former President Dr Sarvepalli Radhakrishnan and others

Prime Minister Jawaharlal Nehru witnesses the Prime Minister's XI vs President's XI Cricket Match, in 1953

The Maharaja (centre) courts arrest after resigning from the Lok Sabha in protest against the merger of Seraikela-Kharsawan, at Cuttack on 29 June 1956

(Left to right) Former president, Dr Zakir Husain, former governor of Orissa, Ajudhia Nath Khosla, and the Maharaja

The Maharaja (left) being sworn in as deputy chief minister of Orissa in 1959

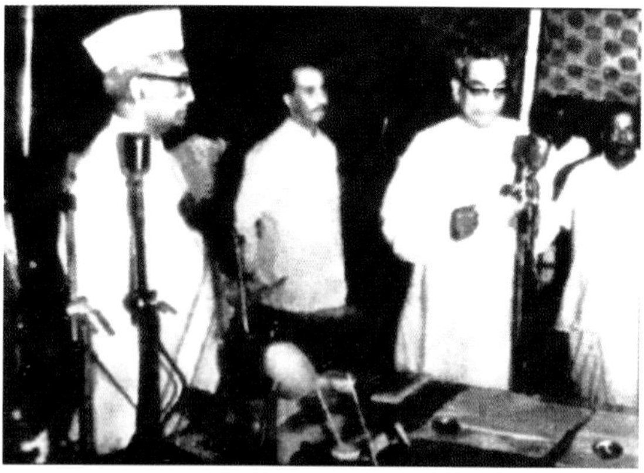

The Maharaja being sworn in as the chief minister of Orissa in 1967

A picture of the Maharaja and Maharani of Patna alongside their Guru Swami Sri Sri Sri Siva Bala Yogi Maharaj and Swamiji's mother

Former CM and renowned statesman Biju Patnaik (centre) at the Maharaja's funeral procession

Narayan resolved to defy the imposition of Section 144. Early in the morning, Rajendra Narayan met with Nilamani Routray, the deputy minister of home affairs, and requested him to withdraw the prohibitory order. Routray did not relent.

The next day, Rajendra Narayan led a procession while walking in the middle of the road. The police were prepared for this. As they marched on, an officer on duty read out a brief declaration informing them that they were defying the prohibitory orders and were sent to the Lal Bagh police station. The dissenters, along with Rajendra Narayan, were thrown into the Cuttack Central Jail. It was extraordinary for a Maharaja, who once held judicial powers, to be jailed. The impact was widespread. More students from across the state came out to defy the prohibitory orders.

Upon getting bail, the Maharaja addressed a historic session of the Utkal Sammilani at Shahid Bhawan, Cuttack. The session continued for two days. Fiery speeches were delivered. Orissa was charged with feverish excitement. There was a massive public meeting at the conclusion of the session. This was unprecedented for any Maharaja. He had created history by resorting to civil disobedience and even courting arrest at the hands of a civilian government as a former member of the privileged monarchy.

The issue of language and several districts falling into states outside of Orissa is an important issue for the people of the state. Therefore, no English language documentation of the history of the state would be complete without acknowledging the cause and sentiments of the people of Orissa that remain deep rooted into their politics and their relations with neighbouring states to this day.

It may be also mentioned that the Congress government at the Centre and the state from 1956 to 1968 did not raise its voice in favour of the remerger of Seraikela with Orissa.

In 1967, with the installation of the first non-Congress government in Orissa and, in fact, in the whole of India, the Orissa Assembly under the leadership of Rajendra Narayan, who became the CM, adopted a resolution demanding the return of Seraikela to Orissa. The resolution was forwarded to the Centre, which was, by then, under the leadership of a powerful PM. Indira Gandhi was not keen on reopening this issue, which was, by then, considered a can of worms.

Another attempt was made for the reunification of the lost districts of Orissa. On the eve of the formation of Jharkhand, Biju Patnaik who was then Orissa CM wrote to Home Minister S.B. Chavan in 1992 and again in 1993. But, the lost districts remain outside of Orissa to this day, with their jurisdiction lying with the newly created state of Jharkhand.

We can now return to the story of the erstwhile Maharaja as a parliamentarian.

Unlike the other maharajas, who entered active politics after the merger, Rajendra Narayan went on to become a leader of the people, one who made an indelible mark on the idea of India, which was gathering world attention. The next chapter charts his progress from the comfort of the palace into the tumble of public life.

5

Palace to Parliament

Politics in Orissa has remained a tumultuous affair throughout history. Odias have carried their identity and heritage with pride. Even today, the Odia identity and culture have stood the test of time despite the people being governed under different Indian states outside of mainland Orissa. Until the merger of the princely states, politics in the Orissa region had consisted mainly of the Congress party, with leaders such as Pt Godabarish Mishra and the Maharaja of Parlakhemundi Sir Krushna Chandra Gajapati Narayana Deb playing a major role. However, it was only when Dr Mahatab entered the fray that the Congress in Orissa witnessed widescale popularity. Dr Mahatab led the salt satyagraha from Orissa in Balasore. By the time of the merger, he had consolidated his position as a formidable Congress leader in the state. As a result of the merger, the Congress absorbed some of the leaders who had led the agitation against the princely states.

After the merger, the state of Patna had merged into the Union of India and a new district named Balangir was created by combining the former states of Patna and

Sonepur.[94] The merger had jolted the rulers out of power and prestige. No longer did the flags emblazoned with royal insignia flutter proudly on the ramparts of their palaces. No more did hundred hands rise in salutation to the maharajas. The mountains had been levelled with the valleys. Unable to reconcile themselves to the changed circumstances, some of the now erstwhile maharajas maintained a lonely distance. To many of those, the paradigm shift was the beginning of adapting to a new reality, for which most were ill-prepared. The maharajas weren't alone—independent democracy was new, even to the common citizens of India. Under the new administration, far away from the reign of their Maharaja, the people of Orissa had begun to feel abandoned and aggrieved.

For the erstwhile ruler of Patna, the boundaries of Balangir had melted. Rajendra Narayan always carried with him the sense that he was not born to be a ruler, and that kept him grounded. The merger was a widening of his canvas for public service. After the lapse of paramountcy and the merger of the princely states into the Union of India, the praja had become the raja. An opportunity had presented itself to serve all of Orissa and India. The former Maharaja knew that 40 per cent of Orissa's population consisted of tribes, wielders of bows and arrows. As a result, the bow and arrow were chosen as the official symbol of the GP.

The Congress party, aware of the upcoming political challenge, downplayed the rise of the Parishad. Perhaps, including some of the erstwhile princes within the Congress fold could have served as a better strategy against an opposition, but the inclusion of the praja mandal[95] leaders into the

[94]Sonepur eventually became a separate district in 1993.

[95]The Praja Mandal leaders openly led agitations against the princely states in the years running up to Independence in 1947.

Congress had complicated matters. The rise of the GP under Rajendra Narayan could not be ignored, and even PM Nehru acknowledged the Parishad, describing it as a party of the Adivasis. The well-being of the poor was the primary focus of the party. It began recruiting volunteers and party workers. Plans and programmes were prepared. Talking points were drafted and printed for the workers. Training was carried out at the Sailashree Palace, where newly recruited party workers were trained in the processes of nomination, election, counting of votes and publication of results. In due course, a few local leaders had emerged from the party. The Parishad's first electoral test was to be in the Lok Sabha Elections of 1951–52.

CONTESTING ELECTIONS

It was on 26 January 1950 when the territorial map of Orissa was redrawn with 13 districts in place of six.[96] The new districts were Balangir, Phulbani, Dhenkanal, Kalahandi, Keonjhar, Mayurbhanj and Sundargarh. As a result of the amalgamation of the princely states, the area of Orissa had doubled. The population had increased by one and a half times of the original. The number of seats in the Assembly went up to 140. The Constitution of India had been framed and India was declared a quasi-federal democratic republic. On the finalization of the constituencies on the basis of universal adult franchise, the country would go to the polls, the first of its kind in the world's largest humanitarian and democratic experiment. It was the first general election of the country. With the introduction of constitutional democracy, which inter alia guaranteed individual right of association, free

[96]The princely states were merged into Orissa resulting in an addition of seven new districts for administrative convenience.

movement, freedom of expression and personal liberty—there was excitement all over the country.

In March, the Election Commission was set up and the Representation of People Act, 1950, was passed in Parliament. It took the next six months, among delays, for Sukumar Sen, ICS, India's then chief election commissioner (CEC) to prepare for the elections, which, apart from being the country's first, would also become the largest election conducted in the world at the time.

By the end 1950, Sardar Patel had passed away, leaving behind an impressive political legacy and his own name cemented in the destiny of independent India as the iron man or lauh purush. Patel's demise also ended his ideological differences with Nehru. Both leaders, being thorough gentlemen, had never attempted to subvert or disrespect one another over their political views. Patel himself respected Mahatma Gandhi's wishes to appoint Nehru as his successor. Nehru's own supporters within the Congress could now secure their hold over the party after Patel.

The general elections took place between October 1951 and February 1952. The GP, which was, formed just a year earlier, won six seats in Parliament. Rajendra Narayan won his Lok Sabha seat with an impressive margin, but the celebrations had to wait. The Assembly elections were to be conducted just a month later. The party leaders and cadres were asked to continue campaigning.

The result of the Assembly elections held in March 1952 proved the former Maharaja's popularity and the success of a credible opposition to the Congress in the state. It was no small success; the GP had won 31 seats from the Garjats. It would become the main opposition party in the Assembly and a leader from the Parishad could become the leader of the Opposition in the House. With 67 seats, the Congress became the single largest party in the Assembly, but failed to obtain an absolute majority. The Socialist Party obtained 10 seats while the Communist Party racked seven seats. The Congress could not win a single seat in Balangir and Keonjhar.

The Congress eventually managed to form the government with the support of five independent candidates. Rajendra Narayan's first foray into electoral politics had been a successful experiment. His victory had proven that he was still alive in the hearts of the people he had served as maharaja. The victory over all nine seats in Balangir established the credibility of the GP.

RULE OF THE PEOPLE IN PARLIAMENT

Knowing fully well that Lok Sabha would not be a walk in the park, Rajendra Narayan tumbled into the fray. The Lok Sabha was a one-party, one-man affair with Nehru at the helm like a colossus. It was precisely for this reason that Rajendra Narayan preferred the Lok Sabha to the state legislative Assembly. His objective was ganatantra—rule of the people—which, he believed, must be established in Parliament, where the Congress enjoyed an overwhelming majority. If democracy must survive, then Parliament was the right place to begin. It was in Parliament where the erstwhile Maharaja brushed shoulders with visionary stalwarts like Dr Rajendra Prasad, S. Radhakrishnan, Krishna Menon, Govind Ballabh Pant, Kailash Nath Katju and Hari Vishnu Kamath.

The first session of the Lok Sabha commenced in May 1952. Freedom fighter Ganesh Vasudev Mavlankar or Dadasaheb, as he was popularly called, was the elected Speaker. One by one, the members of the Lok Sabha stood up to greet each other. Rajendra Narayan welcomed the Speaker, saying, 'Only they on whom fall the Speaker's eyes are fortunate enough to participate in the deliberations of this august house. His eyes naturally fall on the treasury benches, but he needs a third eye for the Opposition.'[97] He had scored his point. A member in the British House of Commons resigns from the party on his election as Speaker and becomes a non-party man. In India, however, the Speaker hails from the ruling party. So there is every possibility of his ruling being influenced by the party in power. Hence the need for a third eye, known as the eye of wisdom and impartiality.

This was the beginning of Rajendra Narayan's journey to democracy in the Lok Sabha. The GP was the third-largest party in the Parliament. Dr S.P. Mookerjee, former vice chancellor of Calcutta University and minister at the Centre, who resigned in protest against atrocities on Hindus in East Bengal (now Bangladesh) led the Hindu Mahasabha, consisting of only four members. Rajendra Narayan formed National Democratic Front with the help of some independent members and small parties, in consultation with Mookerjee. He also proposed the name of Mookerjee, who was called the Edmund Burke[98] of Indian parliament, as leader of the opposition.

It was Rajendra Narayan's initiative to bring the Hindu Mahasabha, GP, Socialist Party and Republican Party under one umbrella as a credible front to counter the mighty Congress party. As the Hindu Mahasabha had overtones of communalism, Mookerjee at the Kanpur conference rechristened his own movement as the Bharatiya Jan Sangh. Rajendra Narayan and Prafulla Chandra Bhanja Deo attended this conference as members of the Lower House and Upper House, respectively, to witness the birth of this nationalist party.

---

[97]*Parliamentary Debates, House of the People: Official Report,* Vol. 1, Parliament Secretariat, New Delhi, 1952, https://bit.ly/3x8lAcN. Accessed on 6 April 2022.

[98]Edmund Burke was a renowned Irish statesman and philosopher.

SEEKING STATE ALLIANCES

If the National Democratic Front could be formed at the Centre, a similar alliance was possible at the state level. Rajendra Narayan discussed this with other Lok Sabha members like Kamath, Sarangadhar Das and Trilok Singh to explore the possibility of a united opposition in Orissa with the Praja Socialist Party (PSP) formed by J.B. Kripalani, a former president of the Congress, along with Gandhian Acharya Narendra Deva, freedom fighter Basawon Sinha and Jayaprakash Narayan, whose impact on Indian political history later earned him the title of 'Lok Nayak'. On getting their consent, he called a meeting of the top leaders of both parties in Delhi. Sraddhakar Supakar, P.K. Deo, Surendra Mohanty from GP, and Surendranath Dwivedy, Trilok Singh and H.V. Kamath from PSP met in Parliament. While the GP had 31, the PSP had only 10 members in the Orissa Assembly. This would have been the first step towards a limited opposition at the state level, had it materialized.

Dwivedi raised an impractical pre-condition, that the Parishad first dissolve into PSP and then each member apply for membership of the PSP. Dwivedi perhaps anticipated that the PSP may not only lose its importance but also lose its existence once it allied with a party three times larger than it was. The Parishad was strongly entrenched in six out of 13 districts of Orissa. The reaction of Mohanty, who initiated the discussion, was sharp: 'What crime had the Parishad committed so that it would go begging, wearing sacks and smearing ashes?'[99] The discussion stopped.

This goes to show how there was a rapport between parties at the national level, but at the state level, the variance in

---

[99]As told to Pabitra Mohan Nayak in a personal interview.

political strategy and motives worked to the detriment of the larger interest of the province. Had PSP merged with the GP in Orissa, it would have had a positive impact on national politics. During the second general election, Orissa politics would have taken a different turn. The PSP had not comprehended the larger picture.

A NATURAL PARLIAMENTARIAN

Rajendra Naryana played an important role in defending Orissa's interest in debates and discussions in the Parliament as an active and constructive participant. Though married in Punjab, Rajendra Narayan raised during the budget session on 20 June 1952, the issue of railway sleepers and import of buffaloes from Punjab for the supply of milk to Punjabi contractors and engineers working on Orissa's Hirakud Dam. He rose to become a resourceful and powerful parliamentarian. 'That is not the way to govern,' he asserted during the thanksgiving to the president's address in 1953, with reference to the Jammu agitation.[100]

Regarding the disparity between the advanced and undeveloped regions of the country, he asked why there was no state-wise comparative statement on development. Digging into the 1951 census report, he questioned the differences in the strength of the Post and Telegraph Departments in Punjab and West Bengal compared with provinces like Bihar, Assam and Orissa where the figures were much lower. He demanded that a superintendent be appointed for the Cuttack

[100]During the Jammu agitation (1949–53), the Jammu Praja Parishad protested against the policies of the National Conference government led by Sheikh Abdullah. The Praja Parishad's call for full integration directly clashed with the demands of National Conference for complete autonomy of the state.

telegraph office and a departmental telegraph office be opened at Sambalpur and the telegraph and money order forms be printed in Odia.

On the Hindu Marriage Bill, tabled on 4 May 1955, he maintained that leprosy should not be deemed ground for divorce, for it may encourage concealment, which is worse than the disease. On the provision that males could not marry for five to seven years after a divorce, he asked, 'Do you expect these human beings to be saints and have no sexual urge during this long period? This undue restriction will drive people into extra-marital relationships and perversion, which is not socially desirable.'[101]

Joining a debate in the same year on scandals about multi-purpose river-valley projects, he said that the Opposition would be much happier if our government did not 'first create scandals and then take the credit for unearthing them.'[102] Pointing out a conflict of interest, he referred to the Hirakud Dam, which was more or less a departmental affair, where the chairman of the Hirakud Dam Control Board was the CM himself.

Accusing the government, Rajendra Narayan observed during a discussion on Representation of the People Bill on 17 May 1956 that no financier ever gives aid without any purpose. He cited the known instance of Orient Paper Mills, Brajrajnagar, which was given a lease of bamboo forests 'at the ridiculously low royalty of four annas per hundred bamboos and provided jeeps, vans and money to the Congress party during the election'.[103]

---

[101]*Parliamentary Debates, House of the People: Official Report,* Vol. 1, Parliament Secretariat, New Delhi, 1955.

[102]*Parliamentary Debates, House of the People: Official Report,* Vol. 1, Parliament Secretariat, New Delhi, 1952, https://bit.ly/3x8lAcN. Accessed on 6 April 2022.

[103]'Rajendra Narayan Singh Deo vs State of Orissa on 17 December 1965, AIR 1966 Ori 214', Orissa High Court, https://bit.ly/3x8hpO3. Accessed on 8 March 2022.

During the discussion on the Second Five-Year Plan on 12 September 1956, he observed that while the per capita income of an agricultural labourer was ₹160 in West Bengal, ₹121 in Punjab and ₹119 in Bihar, it was ₹79 in Orissa. On the other hand, the earnings of an industrial worker in West Bengal, Punjab and Bihar was ₹268, ₹216 and ₹332, respectively, while in Orissa it was ₹145. Asserting that the budget allocation on the basis of population was wrong, he asked why the plan proposal for Orissa was reduced from ₹121.24 crore to ₹62.5 crore and why was there a general budget cut of 5 per cent from all state plans.

QUESTION OF ACCOUNTABILITY

Rajendra Narayan's insistence on a code of conduct for ministers before the election was another significant issue that he raised in Parliament. Referring to the misuse of government vehicles at the time of the election, he said that in the UK even the PM uses private vehicles when he goes on election campaigning. When a Congress MP observed that no allegation against a minister having misused power or exercised undue influence had been brought forward or proved, Rajendra Narayan quoted Raghavachari Krishna Kumar, MP, who had said, 'The fact that no murderers were found or went scot-free does not prove there was no murder.'[104]

Rajendra Narayan also maintained later that party expenditure should not be excluded from the candidate's personal expenditure for the purpose of accountability in elections. Even the expenditure incurred by any individual firm or company in furtherance of the candidates of a party

[104]Discussion in the Lok Sabha on the Representation of People's Bill, 15 May 1956. Parliamentary Archives, India.

should be accountable. Rajendra Narayan had experienced how painful it was to run a party on his own resources, from his privy purse, which was limited to ₹2.56 lakh. For how long could he do so to maintain 'purity of public life', run the party and nurse a career in politics? While the ruling Congress had its Tatas, Birlas and Bilimorias, financing was a major reason why Rajendra Narayan, despite opposition within the party, later merged with the Swatantra Party.

He wanted the ruling party to be right and reasonable, impartial and just. And for this he raised his voice, which was often smothered by the rant, roar and rabble of the party in power. Yet he refused to retreat or retract, whatever the odds. Rajendra Narayan entered Parliament at a time when Orissa was divided and dismembered. Some Odia-speaking tracts were still in the hands of the neighbouring states—West Bengal, Madras, Madhya Pradesh and Bihar. Seraikela, where he was born and which was historically, culturally and linguistically an essential part of Orissa, was forcibly taken away and tagged on to Bihar. As a parliamentarian, he worked for the reunification of Orissa.

STRUGGLE FOR THE LOST DISTRICTS

To the Congress, the party was more important than the province. The voice of Utkal Sammilani to recover and reunite the lost limbs of Orissa had fallen faint. Rajendra Narayan knew that Madhusudan Das, as the founder of Utkal Sammilani, did not join the Congress because it did not help Orissa's reunification. Das also did not join the national mainstream party in order to focus on Orissa's cause. Had he jumped onto the bandwagon, this one-time minister of Bihar and Orissa Province could have found a niche for himself in the higher echelons of the Congress party. Years later, he had another follower in Rajendra Narayan.

While the Utkal Sammilani provided a forum to the former Maharaja, Parliament gave him a platform to fight against the historic injustice of the expropriation of Seraikela to Bihar. Quoting Article 5 of the covenant for the formation of Rajasthan,[105] which stated that the government would ascertain the wishes of the people on whether Bharatpur and Dholpur would remain with Rajasthan or merge with UP, he said this was conveniently forgotten in the case of Seraikela and Kharsawan. There could not and must not be different yardsticks to measure the democratic rights of the people.

Stating in Parliament that the coercive power of the state cannot ensure law-abiding citizens, Rajendra Narayan cited the instance of the government apprehending the secretary of the GP in Koraput on the eve of the election on a false case of instigating a riot, even though on the day of the riot, the secretary was far away from Koraput. He quoted Articles 9, 10 and 11 of Universal Declaration of Human Rights to oppose arbitrary arrest without trial under the Preventive Detention Act.

It had to be admitted, he maintained, that with the forced dismemberment of Odia-speaking regions from mainland

---

[105]The integration of Rajputana states was completed in three stages. The Rajasthan Union was originally formed by the smaller Rajputana states in the southeast, namely Banswara (including Kushalgarh), Bundi, Dungarpur, Jhalawar, Kishengarh, Kotah, Partabgarh, Shahpura and Tonk. These states formed a contiguous area with ethnic, linguistic and cultural affinities. The integration of these states in the contemplated United State of Madhya Bharat was also considered, but it was found that the natural affinity of these states was more with Rajputana than with Madhya Bharat. The territories of these nine states were accordingly united together to form the United State of Rajasthan with an area of 16,807 square miles, a population of 2,334,220 and an average annual revenue of over ₹1.9 crore. The United State of Rajasthan so constituted was inaugurated on 25 March 1948. The larger states of Mewar, Jodhpur, Jaisalmer, Jaipur, Bikaner, etc. joined later.

Orissa, the seeds of disunity, however invisible, had been sown. The discontentment still remained. Referring to the SRC, he said, it was an opportunity for redressing the wrongs of the past and for creating the atmosphere necessary for the harmonious development of the different races in the country bound together by ties of language and culture, each according to its needs and genius, with a common goal.

Raising the issue of the merger of Mayurbhanj with Orissa on 1 January 1949, Rajendra Narayan said,

> It is an ordinary principle observed by courts of law that if a decision is palpably wrong, if a decision is based on a condition and that condition changes, then there is a case for review. Even otherwise, the transfer of Seraikela-Kharsawan to Orissa should have followed a logical consequence. There was calculated repression on Odiya language and culture. Even today, the Odiyas are deprived of the privilege of learning their own language. Was not the election of the GP candidate with an overwhelming majority to the Bihar Assembly a form of plebiscite?
>
> As though the logic of events was inadequate, the people of Orissa are now asked to establish their case for Seraikela-Kharsawan before the SRC. The transfer of Seraikela-Kharsawan to the jurisdiction of the political agent of the Orissa states and the All India States Peoples' Conference further proves the sense of unity with Orissa. In this political upsurge, Bihar had no share. It had no community of interests with the people of Orissa states.

The arguments Rajendra Narayan advanced were neither wrong, nor false. They were irrefutable. Both Nehru and Home Minister Govind Ballabh Pant could not put across strong counters. Appreciating Nehru's neutral stand, Rajendra Narayan said,

> It mattered little to the Government of India whether one bit of territory is in this state or in that state. But while we appreciate the argument that a bit of territory is not running out of India and going into Pakistan or to any other foreign territory, the reason why there is discontent is that this argument is applied against only one particular state. There cannot be double standards, one for Bihar and one for Orissa.[106]

On 2 August 1956, during a discussion on the SRC report, Rajendra Narayan observed that the proposal for a zonal council to settle interstate disputes would not be effective. In a council, there may be three to five states. If two stick to their ground, the others may not intervene. Sometimes one of the states involved in a dispute may fall into a different zone. Then there would be interzonal meetings. This will not solve problems. In light of this, he moved an amendment in the floor of Parliament:

> If any state is dissatisfied with the recommendations of the zonal council in regard to border disputes or linguistic minorities, and represents to the Government of India for appointment of a boundary commission or for arbitration, the Government of India shall appoint a boundary commission or tribunal consisting of judges of the Supreme Court or High Courts for investigation into and adjudication upon such representation and the Government of India shall take necessary steps to implement the award of such commission or tribunal as the case may be.[107]

---

[106] *Lok Sabha Debates on the Report of the States Reorganisation Commission, 14th December to 23rd December, 1955,* Lok Sabha Secretariat, Vol. 1, 1956.
[107] Ibid.

But Parliament had no patience. It fell through. Even an appeal went unheeded, and the Centre had decided not to renew the controversy.

Having lost a formidable battle in Parliament for the cause of Seraikela and Kharsawan, Rajendra Narayan announced on 12 September 1956 the decision of his party to resign from the Lok Sabha, and said, 'While the bold decision of the House on states reorganisation will fulfil the hopes and aspirations of many parts of the country, that day will be a day of mourning for Orissa. It is not possible for us to associate ourselves with this injustice that has been meted out to Orissa in the States Reorganisation Scheme.'

Following the negative report of the SRC relating to Orissa, Rajendra Narayan resigned from Parliament in November 1956. He was then elected to the Orissa State Legislative Assembly in 1957, an era that heralded coalition politics in the country as we shall see in the next chapter.

6

Politics and Statecraft

A new world order was emerging. The Second World War had ended and colonization around the world was ebbing. When independence swept across Africa and Asia, only a handful of the newly freed nations managed to steer themselves out of chaos and autocracy. There was considerable scepticism from the industrialized nations towards these new nations of the world, most of who were heading towards being ruled by dictators. India was different.

Following independence from colonial rule, India had already managed a successful first general election. The INC had emerged as a dominant political force, made even more powerful in the absence of a credible opposition, and reorganized Indian states largely on linguistic lines. Democracy was, however, still new to India, as was its identity as a Union of States, even though the politics of the country was beginning to settle down. By 1957, independent India was ready to vote in second general elections, 100 years after the First War of Independence that had forced Her Majesty's government to take direct control of India and 200 years after Robert Clive[108] established Company Raj in India.

The Constituent Assembly was aware of the plural nature of Indian society and multi-party parliamentary democracy was a natural choice. The first general election was a referendum on the PM and the ruling party. No doubt, the second would go the same way, but regional politics and politicians were rising and beginning to understand the ground realities of a new paradigm.

RISE OF AN OPPOSITION

The Dravidian movement of the south, led by Erode Venkatappa Ramasamy, revered as Periyar[109], had acquired a political identity in the form of the Dravida Munnetra Kazhagam (DMK). The communists were making credible progress in Kerala.[110] Yet, the influence commanded by the Congress at the Centre would remain unchallenged for another few decades. The states were, however, scripting their own distinct narrative. Indian politics at the state level was becoming more decentralized, leading to the rise of non-Congress leaders, activists and parties who would later combine to form joint oppositions and even government. This was the dawn of coalition politics in independent India.

---

[108]On 23 June 1757, Robert Clive's forces leading the British East India Company established their first decisive victory against Nawab Siraj-ud-Daulah and his French allies. Nawab Siraj-ud-Daulah was murdered and the British installed His Commander Mir Jafar Ali Khan Bahadur as the next Nawab of Bengal.

[109]Erode Venkatappa Ramasamy a.k.a Thanthai Periyar founded the Dravidar Kazagham or 'Self Respect' Movement of the Dravidians.

[110]By 1957, E.M.S. Namboodiripad had become the first communist leader in India to head an elected government in Kerala.

In the east, the Seraikela imbroglio that dominated the political scene of Orissa for the first decade of India's independence had been stilled and sealed. It was a deeply emotional issue for both Odias and their leaders. The border movement had ended without a satisfactory resolution. Rajendra Narayan had been elected to the Lok Sabha and raised the border issue, but in vain. Dejected, he had resigned and returned to Orissa, as many other battles loomed before him for the welfare of the state and its people. Back home, the discontentment on the border issue had spilled over towards the leadership. A pamphlet had been published titled *Brihattara Utkala Gathanare Badhabighna* [Hurdles on the path of building a greater Orissa], where the blame was laid squarely at the door of father and son—Aditya Pratap, Raja of Seraikela, and Rajendra Narayan, erstwhile maharaja of Patna—whose contribution to the boundary movement was without measure.[111] Their political rivals had seized an opportunity. The GP, having left Parliament, needed to retain their influence in the state. The party commissioned effective counter propaganda and worked hard to maintain their relations with the people, whose anger over the border issue had by then veered over towards the leadership.

The second general election of 1957 and the legislative Assembly elections in Orissa were conducted simultaneously. With only three other national parties in the fray—Communist Party of India (CPI), Bharatiya Jan Sangh and PSP—the Congress swept the Lok Sabha elections with a winning majority of 371 out of 494 seats at the Centre[112] and reinstated

---

[111]The pamphlet is in possession of Pabitra Mohan Nayak.

[112]*Statistical Report on General Elections, 1957, to the Second Lok Sabha,* Vol. 1, Election Commission of India, New Delhi, https://bit.ly/3MDOeXG. Accessed on 2 May 2022.

Jawaharlal Nehru as the PM, which marked his second term. Winning wasn't as easy for the Congress.

ORISSA'S COALITION POLITICS

On the state legislative front in Orissa, there were 140 seats representing 101 constituencies with 517 candidates in the fray. The Congress and the GP were the largest parties in the state to contest. The results, although close, went in favour of the Congress that bagged 56 of the 140 seats, while the GP won 51 seats. Compared with the first state elections, however, the Congress seat tally came down from 67 to 56 while the Parishad's had risen from 31.[113] For both, the Congress and the Parishad, an opportunity had presented itself to form a government in the state as a coalition.

The other parties in the state elections were the CPI and the PSP. These parties won nine and 11 seats, respectively, while the remaining 13 seats went to independent candidates. It was a hung Assembly.[114] No party had a clear majority. The key political figures in this election were Mahatab and Biju Patnaik from Congress, Dibakar Patnaik and Dwivedi from PSP, besides Rajendra Narayan and Pratap Kesari Deo, erstwhile rulers of Patna and Kalahandi, respectively, from the GP. Loknath Choudhury, Harihar Das and Govinda Pradhan represented the CPI among others.

Although, the Congress had the maximum number of seats, it remained a divided house from within. Biju Patnaik was emerging as a political force within the party, whose sharp

---

[113]*Statistical Report on General Election, 1957, to the Legislative Assembly of Orissa,* Election Commission of India, New Delhi, https://bit.ly/39xdDnR. Accessed on 2 May 2022.

[114]Ibid.

negotiation skills played a key role in cultivating political alliances to support the Congress and increase the tally of its winning coalition to 70 seats. The popular sentiment, however, seemed tilted to favour a non-Congress government.

Had the Opposition managed to set aside its differences and interpersonal rivalries during this election, there could have been a non-Congress government in Orissa, the first in its history. Despite the hectic political activity following a hung Assembly, the Opposition camp failed to arrive at a consensus. The GP and PSP negotiations at Cuttack between Rajendra Narayan, Kesari and Dibakar Patnaik failed to arrive at a common minimum programme[115] offered at the insistence of Surendranath Dwivedi, leader of the PSP in the state. Similarly, the leaders from all parties approached the CPI for support. The deliberations lasted several hours, but the tide was turned by Biren Mitra, the Congress candidate from Cuttack city, who managed to secure the support of the CPI for the Congress. Mitra had been a communist before joining the Congress. Mahatab preserved his credibility by forming a government as CM for the second time. The new government was sworn in on 6 April 1957 amidst unproven allegations of horse-trading and unethical means to garner coalition support.[116] The opposition leaders had not managed to secure support to form a government, the Rajya Sabha elections were the next battlefield.

---

[115]Indian political coalitions often agree on a common minimum programme (CMP) of governance before announcing their collaboration to form government. CMP serves as the de facto manifesto for a government run by a coalition of political parties.

[116]Sarangi, Suresh Prasad, 'The Role of R.N. Singh Deo in the State Politics of Odisha in the Pre and Post-Independent Political Scenario: A Critical Study', *Odisha Review,* pp. 32-33, https://bit.ly/3jbwc2w. Accessed on 8 March 2022.

A RATTLED GOVERNMENT

The Rajya Sabha elections were held on 24 March 1958. There were three vacancies. Harihar Patel from the GP, Diwakar Patnaik from PSP and Bibhudendra Mishra from the Congress won. The other Congress contestant Mohammed Hanif lost on account of cross-voting. The Cabinet viewed this as a debacle, and anticipating a row in the Assembly, deliberated to resign after the Budget Session. The budget however, managed to be passed; the Cabinet did not resign as it would have given the Opposition another attempt to try and form the government. Yet, there was no denying that a political storm was brewing.

One month after the budget session on 24 April 1958, CPI leader Harihar Das, suddenly brought a cut motion. A cut motion is a power given to elected members of the Lok Sabha to oppose a demand in the financial bill discussed by the government. In essence, if a cut motion is adopted by the House, the government will have to prove its numbers on the floor. This makes it a vital tool to test the strength of a government. Following the CPI's cut motion in the House, there was intense lobbying. Three Congress legislators and seven Parishad members crossed the floor.[117] There was turmoil in the Assembly.

Assembly member Mochiram Tiria from the GP, who had been under treatment for tuberculosis in hospital, was brought on a stretcher into the Assembly to vote. The Congress swung into damage control—six of their MLAs were kept under surveillance at Bihari Bag, the Prajatantra office building in Cuttack. The results in the Assembly were staggering—63

[117]In a parliamentary and assembly system in India, parties usually vote as a team, with all party members voting the same way. A member of a party who votes against their party in a division is said to have crossed the floor.

from Congress and 62 from opposition.[118] The Congress managed to pacify the CPI and consequently the latter that had decided to support a non-Congress government, swung back and voted for it. The government was rattled.

Two days later on 26 April 1958, the Congress candidate from Nuapada, Raja Anup Singh Deo of Khariar, publicly declared that he had decided to support a non-Congress government in the state. His colleagues Mohan Naik and Ghasiram Majhi followed suit and resigned from the Congress. The party's hold over their MLAs had clearly weakened. With a wafer-thin margin in the House, the Opposition could soon have had yet another chance at forming the government, had they managed to settle their differences.

Soon thereafter, the Congress Legislature Party met at Bhubaneswar and resolved to vote for the appropriation bill of the 1958–59 Budget. An appropriation bill enables the government to withdraw funds for use from the Consolidated Fund of India[119]. Putting up a bold face, CM Mahatab proclaimed at a press meet. 'After the recent events, the Congress Assembly Party is now stronger than ever and internal dissensions have disappeared.'[120] This proved to be untrue.

The same day Rajendra Narayan and Rabindra Mohan Das (of the PSP) declared that the two parties would work together on a common minimum programme: 'In the context of the present situation, the mere defeat or survival of the Congress party has become immaterial. To break the stalemate is our immediate concern. What is required, therefore, is a

[118]Orissa Legislative Assembly Archives, 1958.

[119]Consolidated Fund of India is defined as the most important of all government accounts. Revenues received by the government and the expenses made by it, excluding the exceptional items, are all part of the consolidated fund.

[120]Orissa Legislative Assembly Archives, 1958.

well-disciplined, progressive and useful party of men who can forget their past prejudices and forge a new political force in the state.'

The very next day, the appropriation bill was put to vote. The ruling party managed to scrape through the division on a 68–66 victory. As a result, in view of other mismanaged incidents by the sitting CM, the Congress Parliamentary Board decided that Mahatab should resign. Mahatab accepted this decision and sent in his letter of resignation to Governor Yashwant Narayan Sukthankar, a retired ICS officer who had earlier served as Cabinet secretary under PM Nehru; asking him to dissolve the Assembly under Article 174 of the Constitution of India.[121] Around this time, there were whispers in the corridors of power that a coalition government comprising of the Congress and the GP could be in the offing. This buzz, however faint, had already created a flutter in political circles.

AN ODD SITUATION

On 11 May 1958, Rajendra Narayan, who had consulted and secured the support of a large portion of the opposition parties, requested the governor to accept Mahatab's resignation before he invited the Opposition to form the government. He further informed the governor that those who had deserted the Parishad earlier, now wished to return to the parent party, but they were being forcibly confined at Bihari Bag, Cuttack and other places for which he should initiate steps so that they could make a free choice.

Governor Sukthankar responded to Rajendra Narayan saying it was not possible to invite the Opposition to form

[121] 'Article 174, Sessions of the State Legislature, prorogation and dissolution', Constitution of India, https://bit.ly/3KglsMc. Accessed on 8 March 2022.

the government in view of the CM's claim that he had the majority. He, however, asked Rajendra Narayan to prove his majority support within 24 hours.

It was an odd situation, which Rajendra Narayan acknowledged in a response to the governor. How could a governor not accept the letter of resignation knowing that the steps to form an alternative government could be initiated only after its acceptance? He also alleged that the governor, instead of meeting the president of India, had met the top brass of the Congress party instead, which was unconstitutional. He further alleged that the governor was helping a discredited ministry and hindering the formation of an alternative government. Countering Mahatab's claim of a majority even after his resignation, Rajendra Narayan wrote:

> …a government resigning office in spite of a majority is not unknown. In 1940, Chamberlain had resigned from office even though his government survived with a slender majority. It may be recalled in this context that the manipulated majority which sustained the Mahatab ministry in office has given rise to serious misgivings in the minds of the people at large. In deference of the moral conscience of the nation, the Congress High Command has directed Mahatab to resign. And yet he has been kept in power. Thus the voluntary abdication of office, perched precariously on the precipice of a doubtful majority in continuous flux was essentially a moral issue. But I regret to submit that non-acceptance of the resignation of the Mahatab ministry straightway frustrated that noble gesture. I am not aware of a ministry resigning on the ground of having lost its moral sanction, yet continuing in office and its leader being again called upon to form a ministry without facing elections. Under the circumstances, the

> continuance of the present ministry by the resigning leader is unprecedented. It would have been unexceptionable had Mahatab and his Council of Ministers continued as a caretaker ministry after his resignation which would have cleared the political atmosphere.

Referring to the governor's request to clearly state the names of those MLAs who supported him, Rajendra Narayan said that the situation was so volatile that it was not possible to spell out the names of his supporters. He alleged that certain members of GP from Phulbani and Mayurbhanj detained in Bihari Bag have been prevented from contacting him. He claimed the support of 72 MLAs whose names, according to him, it was not wise to divulge.

The delay in acceptance of Mahatab's resignation gave the Congress enough time for damage control. It hit back hard. The two MLAs, Naik and Majhi, who had resigned alongside Raja Anup Singh withdrew their resignations. Raja Anup Singh, too, returned to the Congress. Other MLAs who had also abandoned the Congress were forced to beat a hasty retreat.

The governor was in constant communication with the Centre. He did not budge an inch despite Rajendra Narayan's arguments. He did not accept Mahatab's resignation. That very day he asked Mahatab if he could withdraw his resignation, to which he agreed. The saga ended and Mahatab continued as CM, unaware that more drama was yet to unfold, that would change Orissa politics forever, as we shall see in the next chapter.

7

Biju Patnaik's Intervention

On one quiet evening of May 1958, after the political dust had apparently settled in the state, Biju Patnaik's car stopped before the official residence of Raja Bir Udit Pratap Shekhar Deo of Gangpur, who was GP's MLA from Sundergarh. Biju entered the drawing room with a broad smile and without hesitation said, 'Gangpur[122], we had an unpleasant meeting, let's have a drink and shake hands.' They had quarrelled earlier around the time of Raja Anup Singh's resignation. The Raja, being a good sport, felt amused and without a murmur sat down with Biju. They spoke till midnight. That meeting would serve to change the direction of Orissa politics.

Biju was on a mission. The Congress leadership had given serious thought to the issue of merging with the GP, triggering a debate within the party. Biju Patnaik was skilled at making friends, and the meeting with the Gangpur Raja was a

[122]Erstwhile maharajas were commonly addressed by the name of the princely state over which they had ruled. It is done even today. Rajendra Narayan was thus addressed as Patna.

clear message to the Parishad leadership. The Congress high command had been sceptical initially, but Biju succeeded in convincing them. Nehru even went on to cryptically announce during the Durgapur session of the party in May 1959 that the Parishad had to accept the socialistic pattern of society because of the large number of Adivasi membership in the party, even though he doubted whether the rajas would accept it. This was a subtle signal to a changing mindset within the party. Biswanath Das, the president of the Utkal Pradesh Congress Committee, protested. He was not in favour of the Parishad, a fact he disclosed later when he became governor of UP.[123]

The idea of this seemingly strange coalition had germinated in Patnaik's mind. Surendra Mohanty recollected, 'Biju Patnaik was willing to form a coalition with the Parishad. Without any apparent context, he told me, "Surendra! No solution without a coalition."'[124]

To this, Mohanty asked, as though he was prepared, 'Which party, do you think, the Parishad should align with? Is the Congress willing?'

'Come along with Patna for lunch at my residence,' Biju suggested.

'I shall ask Patna,' said Mohanty.

When Mohanty asked the Maharaja, he replied rather indifferently, 'Either way, we will be having lunch, so why not with Biju!'

On the appointed day, the Maharaja arrived with Mohanty at Anand Bhawan, Biju's Cuttack residence. But they were surprised to find Mahatab with senior minister, Lingaraj Panigrahi. Mahatab and Panigrahi asked the Maharaja how would he like the Congress and the Parishad aligning. 'Not

---

[123]As told to Pabitra Mohan Nayak in a personal interview.

[124]This was told by Surendra Mohanty to Pabitra Mohan Nayak.

a bad idea!' the Maharaja responded, but remained silent thereafter.

Biju redoubled his efforts to obtain the final nod from the Congress high command. Each side had its own political objectives. Mahatab wanted to make inroads into the hill tracts, riding on the back of the Parishad, while Maharaja Rajendra Narayan was planning to expand influence in the coastal areas with the help of the Congress.

The idea of a coalition with the Congress did not go well with some leaders of the Parishad too. Pratap Kesari had serious reservations, but Maharaja Rajendra Narayan's view prevailed. It was aligned with his objectives: to save Orissa from political instability, save politics from the impact of money and muscle power and make the Parishad a pan-Orissa party.

SHAPING THE COALITION

The proposal, mooted in May 1958 at the Gangpur Raja's drawing room, took a year to mature. Political stances had changed. The government was at its weakest. Moreover, Biju Patnaik's influence within the state had grown formidably. The idea of a coalition with the Parishad was now gathering steam within the Congress, which meant that support for a feeble government with the CPI as a partner was weakening. The Mahatab ministry was eventually defeated by a narrow margin in an engineered snap poll[125] in March 1959. It was a symbolic defeat; the Congress knew it would come back with another partner. Rajendra Narayan who was the leader of the Opposition from 1957 to 1959 said that the government

---

[125]A snap election in a parliamentary system is called to capitalize on an unusual electoral opportunity or to decide a pressing issue under circumstances when an election is not required by law or convention.

need not resign. His view was from the perspective that the Opposition was in a position of strength, but left the decision to the CM, who decided to step down.

Mahatab, who had earlier branded the GP as 'a party of rulers and feudal lords' was ultimately compelled to acknowledge it as a force to be reckoned with. The Congress found no option but to strike an understanding with its acknowledged adversary. As the deliberations for a new government progressed, Mahatab wanted to form a ministry with six from the Congress and five from the Parishad, remaining as the CM himself. But Rajendra Narayan imposed a condition: if the CM was already from the Congress party, the number of ministers must be equal from both sides. If not, it will neither be possible, nor honourable on the part of the Parishad to join the coalition. This was formally and firmly communicated to the former CM.

Mahatab then invited the Maharaja to Ekamra Niwas, his Bhubaneswar residence. Upon reaching there with Mohanty, they encountered Raja Sailendra Narayan Bhanj Deo of Kanika, who had also been invited. Bhanj Deo's presence was not a coincidence. Mahatab wanted to suggest that if there was a delay in the decision of the Parishad, he would form a government with independent members like Bhanj Deo. Rajendra Narayan remained firm.

A week later, on 22 May 1959, the coalition government took the oath of office with Mahatab once again as CM; Radhanath Rath from the Congress and Rajendra Narayan from the Parishad were sworn in as Cabinet Ministers. The former maharaja was allocated the portfolios of finance, law and industry. After the swearing-in ceremony, Mahatab and the Maharaja issued a joint statement to the press: 'We are determined to put an end to the present unstable condition for the realization of our cherished goal of a great and prosperous

India in which Orissa will play a distinguished role.'[126]

The entire rejig of the government was due to the background laid by Biju Patnaik; he had not only managed to strengthen the government, but also brought a powerful opposition to support it; Biju's role and outstanding negotiation skills were no doubt responsible for several paradigm shifts in Orissa's politics later. Both Biju and Mahatab served as CMs of Orissa, but their political careers progressed very differently. Mahatab, who had been a part of the Dandi March Satyagraha of Mahatma Gandhi as well as the Quit India movement, was also a distinguished writer. He had founded a daily newspaper by the name of *Prajatantra*, which remains in print to this day. Mahatab is fondly remembered by the people as Utkal Keshari.

Biju Patnaik served as CM of Orissa twice; he was a skilled pilot, businessman, freedom fighter and politician. He had even piloted sorties for the Sikh Regiment in the critical military intervention in the state of J&K in 1947, upon the request of PM Jawaharlal Nehru. Biju's keen sense to remain on the right side of history shaped Orissa's political future in the following decades. Biju's legacy as both a visionary and kingmaker enabled an entire generation of Orissa to remember him as one of the tallest leaders in their history. Even during his disagreements with Maharaja Singh Deo, there remained civility and mutual respect. Much the same as the original titans of the Congress party, both Jawaharlal Nehru and Sardar Vallabhbhai Patel did not allow the party and cadre to be adversely affected on account of their ideological differences. A fiercely independent mind, Biju later disagreed with PM Indira Gandhi and joined the movement with Jayaprakash Narayan, being one of the first politicians to be arrested during

[126]Das, Manmath Nath and C.P. Nanda, *Harekrushna Mahtab,* Publications Division, Ministry of Information & Broadcasting, Government of India, 2001.

the Emergency. He remained in public service until his death in 1997. His son, Naveen Patnaik, holds the record for the longest serving[127] CM of the state from Biju Janata Dal, which was named in his honour.

Patnaik's well intentioned and skilfully executed master plan for a coalition between the Congress and the Parishad, designed for the stability and welfare of Orissa was, however, a non-starter as detailed in the next chapter.

> In my dream of the 21st century for the state, I would have young men and women who put the interest of the state before them, who have pride in themselves, confidence in themselves. They will not be at anybody's mercy, except their own selves. By their brains, intelligence and capacity, they will recapture the history of Kalinga.[128]
>
> —Biju Patnaik, 1992.

[127]At the time of writing this book, Naveen Patnaik has also been the second-longest serving CM in India after Pawan Kumar Chamling of Sikkim. Chamling's 25-year stint (1994-2019) as CM leading his party, the Sikkim Democratic Front is the longest ever by a CM of any Indian state.

[128]Biju Patnaik's self note in 1992 in his diary.

8

Death of a Coalition

The new coalition had 111 out of 140 MLAs in the Orissa Assembly. With this strength, no political need would arise to buy votes or smuggle members from other parties. Intended to bring in political stability, however, the coalition government was bedevilled from its very inception. It came into being to end a political crisis and avert the imposition of president's rule besides allowing coalition allies to extend their sphere of political influence. But, 'unity of purpose and unity of action' was a foregone aspiration and the unholy alliance would have broken up within a few days, had it not been for Rajendra Narayan's patience and perseverance that allowed the coalition to continue for three years and 10 months.

Ambition and personality clashes persisted in an atmosphere of suspicion and distrust within the Congress. The coalition itself had several petty unresolved disputes. Both the Congress and the Parishad had locked horns on key ministerial appointments. A bitter rivalry had begun to brew between Biju and Mahatab. Both had become wary of each other's growing influence around the high command, particularly Nehru.

BIJU-MAHATAB DISCORD

While Biju's tenacity had achieved the impossible task of bringing Congress and the Parishad to share from the same plate, Mahatab's suspicion of Biju grew deeper, giving rise to conflict and much drama. Mahatab opposed Biju's suggestion that alongside Biju himself, Nilamani Routray and Biren Mitra— one an influential politician and the other who had outsmarted the negotiations for Congress to prove its majority by winning CPI support—be taken in as parliamentary secretaries, if not as ministers. The CM did not relent and a disgruntled Biju left India on a business trip to Europe two days before the coalition government was ushered in.

Later, Biju wrote to Rajendra Narayan from Calcutta, pleading that his intention was not to sabotage the government, but to show a 'measure of goodwill'. In a letter dated 20 May 1959, Biju wrote to the Maharaja, clearing the air about his intentions to remain part of the government and serve the people.[129] Biju reiterated that a political ploy, already underway, insinuated that Biju was trying to get into the government to sabotage the policies formulated by GP ministers. The situation was indeed murky.

There was no doubt that Biju had worked hard to strengthen the government for it to remain stable and carry out a sound policy implementation. The coalition Cabinet was small. The issue of denying Biju, Biren and Nilamani led to a groundswell of discontentment and dissatisfaction. Biju, having done most of the heavy lifting in making the coalition a reality, was most disappointed. His own political ambitions, justified for any career politician, remained hanging between the CM and the coalition ministers in the small-sized Cabinet

---

[129]A copy of the letter lies with the Maharaja's family.

that had left no ministerial berth vacant.

As a first step, Biju motivated the Congress MLAs to exert pressure for the expansion of the Cabinet. Two months into the coalition, the Congress could not do without expansion. Eight ministers were appointed. This time, too, Biju was kept out. He now staged an open rebellion against CM Mahatab. On 20 February 1960, Biju addressed a letter to Mahatab, alleging that he was becoming self-centric and had forgotten about the party ideologues, who could equally contribute to the honour and efficiency of the party.[130]

Mahatab replied that he had worked as a leader of the Congress for a long time and took responsibility for the stability and strength of the party. In a nutshell, the CM did not budge, which was a snub more so when Biju had worked for more than a decade and remained loyal to the party. The real reason behind this tussle was Mahatab's own standing with the party high command in Delhi, where the image of a CM keeping matters stable in the state would further strengthen his influence. Biju, on the other hand, as a younger and more ambitious politician, had his own image to create amid the central leadership of the party.

IMPOSITION OF PRESIDENT'S RULE

Matters reached a breaking point when by June 1959, Biju asked Mahatab to dissolve the coalition saying he was losing face with the high command. This was a puzzling state of affairs. Keeping the coalition intact would have projected Biju as a non-influential leader in front of the high command and dissolving the coalition would result in a loss of face for Mahatab, who had persuaded the Centre to agree to the

[130]Orissa Government Archives, Bhubaneswar.

coalition. It had become an issue of prestige.

The Parishad watched its coalition partner crumble from within due to the power struggle between two political stalwarts that took place at the cost of the welfare of the people. The quarrel was for power, which has today become the default Indian political format in every state. Further, Orissa had faced severe drought in 1953 and 1954, along with a devastating flood the following year, which had destroyed a considerable portion of Cuttack. It is important to note in this record of Orissa's political history from the point of view of the Rajendra Narayan that the entire political drama for power within the Congress and the differences with their coalition partner were in the years following these natural calamities. Democracy had come to India, but the democratic sentiment was missing.

As the stalemate prolonged, relations were further strained and rapport was ruptured. Unhappy with the situation, the Congress Party formed a sub-committee under the Pradesh Congress Committee (PCC) chief Banamali Patnaik, to examine whether the Parishad should merge with the Congress or the coalition should continue. Mahatab had seen the writing on the wall and knew his days as CM were numbered. Anticipating an unfavourable decision from the committee, he wrote to the then party president Neelam Sanjiva Reddy[131] to relieve him as CM.

Mahatab also informed Rajendra Narayan that he was going to persuade his colleague, Biswanath Das, to take over. Biswanath Das had earlier served as PM of Orissa Province in British India. He was also a member of the Constituent

---

[131]Excellency Neelam Sanjeeva Reddy was the president of the Indian National Congress and later became Speaker of the Lok Sabha and the sixth president of India.

Assembly representing the state of Orissa and had built a reputation for being an extremely bold politician. Rajendra Narayan understood that Das's boldness would cause even further friction with the coalition. He also realized that Mahatab's suggestion for Das was in the interest of a prolonged stalemate and not to achieve an administrative and political balance to ensure that the government could function.

So, the Maharaja responded, 'Since pressure from your side to end the present arrangement as soon as possible is such, as to induce you, to wish to be relieved of your present position, it is difficult for me to visualize how the existing arrangement can continue to fulfil its objective.'[132] The Maharaja was polite, but any skilled diplomat would have read his dissent between the lines.

By the time Mahatab's letter reached the party president, Reddy was on a visit to Himachal Pradesh. PM Nehru was on an official visit to the US, and Morarji Desai, then finance minister, was not in Delhi either. In the meantime, the sub-committee submitted its report, which was duly approved by the PCC. On 20 November 1960, the PCC resolved that 'in the best interest of the state and in furtherance of the best democratic tradition, the coalition ministry should be dissolved conveniently soon after the next annual budget is passed and at least ten months before the general election in February of 1962 in order that the coalescing parties prepare freely for the verdict of the electorate.'[133] The committee further directed the Congress MLAs to approach the governor for the promulgation of president's rule in Orissa till the formation of the next government.

---

[132]Letter from Maharaja's office dispatched on 24 September 1960.

[133]Das, Manmath Nath and C.P. Nanda, *Harekrushna Mahtab*, Publications Division, Ministry of Information & Broadcasting, Government of India, 2001.

By February 1961, a year before the general election was to be conducted, Biju was elected as PCC president. His victory was the party's mandate for the dissolution of the coalition, which he initiated as a formal request to CM Mahatab within a week of taking charge.

Reddy, as party president, finally responded to Mahatab's letter stating that since the Congress Parliamentary Board had empowered Mahatab to form the coalition, it alone could decide to dissolve the government. As a result, the government should convene the Assembly and present the budget. The Congress Parliamentary Board reiterated the views of the party president. The gloves were off. Both Biju Patnaik and Harekrushna Mahatab had a significant support base within the party. Some party workers began mooting the idea of a new Congress government that would take over after the upcoming budget session. Senior members of the party said they were not going to be 'party to indecent manoeuvres for promotion of an alternative Congress government through a manipulated majority'.[134]

Rajendra Narayan, who was then finance minister, sensed this and wrote to Mahatab on 18 February 1961: 'If there is any contemplation for the formation of an alternative government prior to next general election and there is any possibility of earlier dissolution of Assembly and of the midterm election, it would not be proper for us to present or pass the budget. In this context, I would be failing in my duty to myself and my party if I take the responsibility of presenting the budget to the Assembly in an atmosphere of uncertainty.'

By this time Mahatab had lost interest in the coalition, and resigned as the CM taking cognizance of the tremendous political pressure from within his own party. The coalition

[134]Orissa Government Archives, Bhubaneswar.

thus collapsed and president's rule was declared in Orissa for the first time on 25 February 1961. The coalition came to an end because of a fruitless struggle for power between two powerful leaders.

POST-MORTEM OF A POWER STRUGGLE

Premature parting of ways was a moral victory for GP, which had, all throughout, behaved in a dignified manner, displaying its faith in democracy and political decency, thereby attracting the admiration of the people. It might not have weakened the Congress much, but it had completely isolated Mahatab and compelled him to quit the Congress and father a new party, the Orissa Jana Congress, five years later.

The coalition had lasted two years. But it brought to the fore Rajendra Narayan's great regard for democratic ideals and political morality. While Biju and Mahatab were fighting, he remained completely detached and non-partisan. Eventually, Mahatab's influence over the Congress waned. He distanced himself from the party and power.

In hindsight, the death of the coalition was embedded in its birth, sandwiched between two powerful rivals—Harekrushna Mahatab and Biju Patnaik. As early as 30 June 1959, Biju had advised Mahatab to break the coalition. But Mahatab persuaded the Centre to allow him to continue with the coalition. Had he broken it within a few days of its formation, it would have seriously affected his credibility and capability. Moreover, as a seasoned politician, he could smell Biju's increasing influence over the Congress, both at the Centre and the state. Outside the ambit of power, it would have been difficult for him to either confront or contain Biju, who was sharper, younger and more ambitious.

The coalition thus collapsed on account of their power

struggle. The GP was vindicated in its stand for governance, which was visible in the Rajendra Narayan's policies during his brief stint as industries and finance minister. In this time, Rajendra Narayan commissioned several projects in accordance with the Second Five-Year Plan, which Nehru had ambitiously rolled out under the great P.C. Mahalanobis, member of of the Planning Commission. The plan had advocated heavy industrialization, which resulted in Rajendra Narayan launching several hydroelectric, irrigation and electrification projects, including the hydroelectric projects of Hirakud and Machhkund. The revenue receipts as well as the per capita income of the state witnessed positive growth during his tenure as finance minister.

With the collapse of the coalition and imposition of president's rule, the state prepared for midterm polls as we shall see ahead.

9

The Turbulent '60s

Three months into president's rule, it was time to elect a new government. Orissa had passed through many political changes. Metaphorically, much water had flowed down the Mahanadi. The notion of an alternative to a large national party dominating the political scene in the country had crossed people's minds, an idea that would gain strength over the following decades, as history has witnessed. India in the 1950s and 1960s had already witnessed the birth of coalition governments in the states.

The short-lived coalition between the GP and the Congress had collapsed, but the former Maharaja had managed a novel experiment[135]—the marriage of a provincial party with a national political organization. Such coalitions remained a viable political tool within the framework of the constitution for all time to come.

The midterm election to the Orissa Assembly was held

---

[135]The 1954 coalition government in Tamil Nadu, 1957 coalition government in Orissa and the 1960 coalition government in Kerala were among the first coalition state governments in history of independent India.

in 1961. The OPCC braced itself to fight the polls, this time under the leadership of Biju Patnaik. With Mahatab marginalized, Biju prepared to steer the state through a rather uncharted course based on his vision. The state Congress faced no dearth of resources as money was the *amogh astra*, an unfailing weapon in the hands of a powerful national party. The poll campaign drew many Congress leaders, who visited Orissa several times with tall promises if the Congress was voted to power.

No opposition could have matched the massive scale at which Biju conducted the campaign. The Parishad stood dazzled at the spectacle, but their finances had begun dwindling. The former Maharaja had managed to run the party from his own private resources for 12 years.

POLL VICTORY TO BIJU

Biju's leadership had matured and he inspired the people. He urged them not to remain content with what they did not have. He assured them the availability of drinking water, rural electrification and tiled roofs. He fired the imagination of the youth who found in him an unusual hero. He urged them to draw inspiration from his own life; he had risen from humble beginnings to become a millionaire.[136] Biju's rival, Mahatab, expecting the Congress to lose, did not contest the election. He told mediapersons, 'For another decade, the Congress cannot get on without a coalition.'[137] Many Mahatab supporters fought

[136]As a businessman, Biju Patnaik set up various industries—Kalinga Tubes, Kalinga Airlines, Kalinga Iron Works, Kalinga Refractories and *The Kalinga,* a daily Odia newspaper. He also established the international Kalinga Prize for popularization of science and technology in 1951 and entrusted its responsibility to UNESCO.

[137]As retold by A.U. Singh Deo.

as independent candidates. However, the results of the 1961 Assembly elections defied speculation.

On the second day of counting, the Congress and Parishad were neck to neck. Biju expected the Congress score not to exceed 72, but it did. For the first time after Independence, the Congress gained a signal victory over other parties with 82 out of 140 seats.[138] Its performance over the 1957 Assembly elections improved in the coastal belt, from 51 seats to 64 seats and in the hill districts from five seats to 18 seats. The Parishad's tally, on the other hand, went down. It scored 37 seats against 51 in the previous poll. While the Congress bagged 25 more seats, the Parishad were 14 less than in 1957. The CPI was reduced to four, while the PSP managed 10 seats. Although Kalahandi and Sundargarh yielded one seat each to Congress, Balangir, the bastion of the Parishad, stayed invincible in spite of Biju's influence and muscle. Out of the 191 Independents, only seven Independents won, of which four joined the Congress, while the remaining three pledged full support.[139]

The poll outcome held surprises for both the Congress and the Parishad. The Congress had gained from the failure of the Opposition to form a pre-poll alliance and managed to absorb all the losses of the PSP and the CPI. The Parishad sustained the heaviest loss, losing even their safe seats. Top PSP leaders too lost their traditional seats. Only three Independents out of 30 Mahatab loyalists won. The much smaller Jharkhand Party was wiped out. The Congress had won a decisive victory on the back of a heavyweight campaign, resources and Biju Patnaik's promise of a quick uplift.

---

[138]Government of India, *Statistical Report on General Election, 1957, to the Legislative Assembly of Orissa,* Election Commission of India, New Delhi, 1957.
[139]Ibid.

DEVELOPMENT WINS

Biju Patnaik was sworn in as CM in June 1961. He formed a Cabinet with seven ministers and seven deputy ministers. Biren Mitra became deputy CM and Routray was sworn in as civil supplies minister. Once again, Rajendra Narayan became the leader of the opposition and was elected as chairman of the Public Accounts Committee.

The new CM was a quick decision-maker. As an immediate directive of the new government, trade and commerce were urged to run at full throttle. His focus was on building the industrial strength of the state. His dynamism, alongside his closeness to the central leadership, helped to introduce some innovative industrial development in the state like the Talcher thermal power plant and the Balimela hydel project, the work of which were initiated during his tenure. He also contributed to road development.

In 1970, while addressing the annual day celebrations of the Gangadhar Meher College at Sambalpur, Biju recalled his efforts to build the express highway linking Daitari to Paradip, the work of which had been stalled on the issue of land acquisition. Biju then called the chief engineer, Mumtaz Ali, to his office to enquire into the delay and address this issue. Ali explained that a large number of villages and streams were in the way, because of which acquiring the land and making it fit for the highway development was proving to be a mammoth task. Looking at the map of Orissa lying on his table, Biju brought out a red-blue pencil, and drawing a straight line from Daitari to Paradip, said, 'Here is the National Highway.' This highway is still operational today. He also spearheaded the development of the port of Paradip.

Biju was a businessman first, a skilled politician second. Unlike the more subdued demeanour of Mahatab, Biju as

CM appeared self-assured. He liked to work fast and lacked patience with bureaucracy that characteristically wanted to cling to the status quo on policy matters. For most young Odias, the new CM was a dreamer and a visionary, sometimes ruled by whims and fancies. Biju was inclined towards the ends justifying the means, even if the ends sometimes came at the cost of due procedure.

His political contemporary Rajendra Narayan, on the other hand, was more measured and subtle in his approach. Being a Gandhian, he was careful of the means. However, both, Patnaik and Rajendra Narayan, were broad-minded, liberal and generous. While one was impatient, unrestrained and sometimes brazen, the other was calmer, measured, self-restrained and gentle, yet tough and decisive. A Orissa needed Biju's dynamism and Rajendra Narayan's political wisdom coupled with cautious experience and optimism. The differences in their personalities were evident in their dealings with political rivals.

MERGER WITH SWATANTRA PARTY

A few years earlier in 1959, leaders like C. Rajagopalachari, M.G. Ranga and Minoo Masani had formed a new national liberal party known as the Swatantra Party, as a reaction to the Nehru-dominated Congress's socialist outlook. The party was an advocate for free enterprise and allowed its members to be guided by their conscience and convictions. This was a powerful statement and received popular support from princes like Maharawal Chandraveer Singh and Laxman Singh of Banswara and Dungarpur, respectively, and Maharani Gayatri Devi of Jaipur and Maharaj Hukam Singh of Jaisalmer.

In the meantime, even as Biju was in a rush to usher in development in Orissa, financial issues had crippled the

GP, compelling it to search for a national organization with an ideology in congruence with its own. As the policies and programmes of the Swatantra Party were 'remarkably similar', Rajendra Narayan entered into a series of discussions with Rajagopalachari and eventually decided to merge his party with the Swatantra Party in March 1962.

The GP, having formed a formidable opposition to the Congress in the state, was already finding it difficult to manage its own finances. Further, when the partnership between the Parishad and the Congress to form the government abruptly ended, it had left party finances in a critical position, making it difficult to fund another election. The advantage for merging on behalf of the Parishad was therefore not only the support from a section of Indian businesses[140] that the Swatantra Party commanded, but also the political direction of a true liberal alternative, closer to Gandhi's philosophies than even the Indian National Congress. The Maharaja reasoned that a merger with the Swatantra Party would bring a significant portion of the middle-class and the princes that constituted the Parishad to support the Swatantra Party. The idea that every major voice of dissent against the ruling Congress at the Centre would unite was a powerful one. The GP was one of the most significant mergers to the Swatantra Party along with the Janata Party of Bihar. Rajendra Narayan was nominated into the executive committee of the Swatantra Party.

It was a critical time for India. By 1962, the political scenario was beginning to change, both domestically and globally. The Cold War was brewing. A secret agreement between Soviet Union's Nikita Khrushchev, Cuba's Fidel Castro and the Cuban revolutionary Che Guevara led to a build-up of Soviet

[140]In respect and courtesy for an unofficial request, the authors have expunged the names of business houses mentioned in this paragraph.

ballistic missiles on the island nation of Cuba, which was a deterrent against the failed Bay of Pigs invasion of 1961. The US president, John F. Kennedy addressed the nation promising a full retaliatory response upon the Soviet Union leading to the Cuban Missile Crisis. With the Soviet Union looking the other way, the crisis gave the Chinese Premier Zhou Enlai and Mao Zedong, the president of the Communist Party an opportunity to 'teach India a lesson' amidst the escalating border dispute. The resulting Sino-Indian War was devastating for the nation and raised serious questions on Nehru's legitimacy as a leader. Nehru's health had also begun to deteriorate. An anti-Congress sentiment was building up and that impacted the working of the Orissa state government too.

Biju's government, in its first year, had aimed at rapid industrialization and expansion. However, allegations of fraud and misappropriation of state funds had begun to surface. By the following year, this dissent had begun to spill over into the streets with widespread protests against the government amidst allegations of corruption. Biju's government had merely completed two years when the Maharaja, being both the leader of the Opposition and chairman of the Public Accounts Committee, was asked to enquire into these allegations. In the meantime, the country was gearing up for the general election of 1962.

A TEMPESTUOUS TIME

The debacle of the Sino-Indian War had shaken the government and the ruling Congress party on the ground as well as in Parliament. People were questioning what the party had done since the elections, which was the popular sentiment underlying the 1962 polls. The party had already lost Vallabhbhai Patel; Govind Ballabh Pant had suffered a cerebral stroke in 1961 resulting in his sudden death. Nehru's illness had made him increasingly unavailable. Yet, Nehru once again won a landslide victory in his third and final election campaign. The Congress won 361 of the 494 seats.[141] The Congress was back in power. However, given his failing health and inability to function effectively, Nehru asked Madras CM K. Kamaraj to take over as president of the party in October 1963.

The new chief of the Congress party had a radical plan—he was of the firm belief that being in power, party leaders had increasingly become complacent. He swiftly asked all senior leaders at the centre and states to voluntarily resign and join the organizational work on the ground to rebuild the party from the grassroots. The mass resignation, which came to be known as the 'Kamaraj Plan' included Biju Patnaik, who got involved in the work of revitalizing the Congress party. Biren Mitra succeeded Biju as CM. Biju's own vision for rapid industrial growth could be fulfilled as deputy chairman of the State Planning Board, a position offered to him by Biren Mitra[142] after Biju stepped down as CM.

When Nehru passed away in May 1964, Kamaraj was the party's natural choice to succeed as PM. However, faced with the herculean task to hold the party together, Kamaraj declined the post and instead brought Lal Bahadur Shastri, the minister of external affairs, as the new PM.

In the meantime, encouraged by the Chinese attack of 1962, President Ayub Khan of Pakistan launched Operation Gibraltar in an attempt to 'liberate' Kashmir, leading to the Indo-Pakistan War of 1965. Even as Shastri managed the

---

[141]*Statistical Report on the General Elections, 1962 to the Third Lok Sabha,* Election Commission of India, https://bit.ly/3snkyGV. Accessed on 9 May 2022.

[142]A leader of the Congress and the CM of Orissa from 2 October 1963 to 21 February 1965.

war decisively, the ill-conceived Pakistani military intervention worked to unite the country. To formally end the war, PM Shastri visited Uzbekistan to sign the Tashkent Declaration. The following day, he died under mysterious circumstances. Kamaraj then backed Nehru's daughter Indira Gandhi, then the minister of information and broadcasting in Shastri's government, as the new PM, ahead of 1967 general elections.

By the late 1960s, a formidable opposition had organized itself to challenge the Congress party, both at the Centre and the states that included the Bangla Congress of West Bengal under Ajoy Mukherjee, the Bharatiya Kranti Dal of UP under Charan Singh, the Bihar Jana Congress and the DMK of Tamil Nadu. Even Orissa was simultaneously heralding the winds of change.

While Biren, as Biju's replacement was a popular leader, he lacked administrative experience. Although his chief ministership successfully turned the government's focus on growth of education in the state, he did not last long in office. The Orissa University of Agriculture and Technology was established during his tenure. Biren resigned in 1965 and was replaced by Sadashiva Tripathy, then revenue minister. CM Tripathy was a soft-spoken and honest man, but even he did not last in office and had to resign under political pressure in 1967.

Political chaos ensued. The state had witnessed this before. Mahatab, already miffed with the Congress, left the party and constituted a new organization called the Orissa Jana Congress[143] with seven members. They concentrated on the popular anti-Congress sentiment, which was known countrywide as the 'Congress Hatao (Reject the Congress party)' movement. Mahatab had adjusted to the changing

---

[143]Dr Harekrushna Mahatab formed the Orissa Jana Congress along with Pabitra Mohan Pradhan, Banmali Patnaik and Surendra Patnaik. The Orissa Jana Congress merged with the Janata Party in 1977.

political reality. His Orissa Jana Congress was winning support against the INC. Even the Swatantra Party had popular support from all sections that were against an all-powerful state that tightly controlled industry.

The general election of 1967 and the Assembly election of Orissa were conducted together. Besides Mahatab, Chhaudhury and Rajendra Narayan from the Swatantra Party went up against the Biju-Biren combined. There were widespread anti-incumbency and hostile demonstrations. Congress was unable to hold any meeting smoothly. Even Indira, who visited Bhubaneswar on 8 February 1967, was greeted with demonstrations against the Congress.

The elections, once again, brought in the Congress party at the Centre, in its fourth consecutive term, this time under the leadership of Indira Gandhi, who won the people's mandate. In the state Assembly election of Orissa, with a multitude of parties in the fray and discontentment in the Congress, the Swatantra Party won 49 seats, Mahatab's Jana Congress came in with 26 seats, INC managed 31, while the PSP scored 21 seats. The communists too managed a few seats.[144]

The Swatantra Party had succeeded in extending its sphere of influence in the coastal districts. In sharp contrast to the divided Congress House, it was revealed that the Swatantra Party and Mahatab's Orissa Jana Congress had entered into a pre-election alliance on a 21-point programme and formed the government. The alliance had gained an absolute majority of 75 out of 140 seats.[145] Rajendra Narayan, as the chief of the Orissa unit of the Swatantra Party, was chosen to lead the state as the new CM of Orissa, as we shall see in the next chapter.

---

[144]*Statistical Report on General Election, 1967, to the Legislative Assembly of Orissa*, Election Commission of India, https://bit.ly/394IHuK. Accessed on 9 May 2022.
[145]Ibid.

10

Chief Minister Singh Deo

The erstwhile ruler of Patna was sworn in as the CM of Orissa. Rajendra Narayan became the CM of the first non-Congress government in the country following the pre-poll alliance between the Orissa Jana Congress and the Swatantra Party. The oath-taking ceremony took place on 8 March 1967. While Pabitra Mohan Pradhan of the Orissa Jana Congress became the deputy CM, Sadashiva Tripathy, the previous Congress CM, became the leader of the opposition. The CM's Council of Ministers consisted of 13 ministers with six ministers from the Jana Congress and the remaining seven from the Swatantra Party.

The 1967 election was won and lost virtually on a single agenda—corruption. Corruption had slowly become the single biggest agenda in the state involving allegations against CMs and ministers of the past. People were distressed by political instability and in the run-up to the elections, most opposition parties launched an anti-corruption campaign that brought together the coalition to defeat the Congress. The coalition had promised a probe into the alleged corruption charges against ministers in their 21-point common minimum programme. As promised, one of the first steps by the coalition government was to set up a one-man enquiry commission to look into these charges against CMs and ministers between 1961 and 1967. In October 1967, the government appointed Justice Hans Raj Khanna of the Delhi High Court to head this commission.

In the meantime, in June 1967, Tripathy too, had written to President Zakir Husain Khan, a letter signed by 24 MLAs urging an enquiry into the allegations against the ministers, which included the names of Rajendra Narayan, Mahatab, Nabakrushna Choudhuri, Santanu Das and S.N. Patnaik.[146] The Union Home Minister Y.B. Chavan, referred Tripathy's letter to Rajendra Narayan, who, as CM, promptly appointed Justice J.R. Mudholkar of the Supreme Court of India to enquire into the allegations in the interest of integrity in public life.[147] No CM had ever had the courage to institute a commission of enquiry against himself. It was a unique precedence and the erstwhile Maharaja created history in keeping with his clean image.

AN AGENDA FOR CHANGE

The coalition then set to work to establish a clean and stable government in keeping with its 21-point agenda that included ruthless elimination of corruption and nepotism at all levels of government, setting up an institution of the ombudsman for eradication of corruption; increasing administrative efficiency and the rule of law; promoting fair governance free from

---

[146]Misra, G., 'Dr. Harekrushna Mahtab vs The Chief Minister Of Orissa And... on 23 September, 1970', indiankanoon, https://bit.ly/37aZlbO. Accessed on 2 May 2022.

[147]The period between 1967-74 saw four commissions of enquiry by the sitting government against their political adversaries in the state. Odia intellectuals termed this as 'Commission Rajneeti'.

political pressure, instilling discipline and change of outlook in the police force for public service; austerity and avoidance of wasteful expenditure; elimination of unnecessary controls, permits, licences and quotas through a non-political independent statutory board; establishment, expansion and completion of existing universities; abolition of land revenue, reduction of tax burden and elimination of harassment in the collection of state dues; easier procedures for expansion of business and industry for increasing employment; introduction of Odia in a state language administration; development of backward areas and special attention to SC, ST and other backward classes; abolition of panchayat taxes and entrusting panchayats with resources of non-tax revenue thus affecting real decentralization as envisaged in the Constitution of India under Directive Principles of State Policy; liberating primary education from the control of panchayat samitis; expansion of technical and general education with special attention to backward areas; practical development plans for agriculture, provision of basic necessities for the people and provision of infrastructure for economic development; change in the monopoly system in Kendu leaf trade; appointment of a finance commission for enquiry and report on all aspects of the Orissa famine of 1966.

This agenda was implementable within the fiscal ability of the state. Rajendra Narayan's administrative experience as the ruler of Patna, along with his tenure as minister of the state Cabinet, particularly finance, led him to streamline administrative processes and establish a transparent procedure in government, making it more accountable.

WORKING FOR DEVELOPMENT

A new wave of development took over the state. Orissa, during Rajendra Narayan's tenure, became one of the first states in

India to appoint a Lokayukta based on the recommendations of the Administrative Reforms Commission, appointed by the Government of India in 1966 that had recommended setting up an ombudsman in the states for accountable governance. The 21-point agenda was implemented well. In agriculture, the government made provisions for high-yield seeds and expanded irrigation to contribute to the ongoing 'Green Revolution across the country. In education, the government set up new primary schools and brought the number of high schools and middle schools to 5,200. The government also set up 94 ashram schools[148], 13 residential sevashramas, 773 hostels and three training centres for teachers to assist the ashram and sevashram schools.

By 1970, the Rajendra Narayan government had set an impressive governance record. Thirteen tuberculosis centres had been deployed for better healthcare. Mass immunizations had been conducted against diphtheria, whooping cough and tetanus. A minimum wage was fixed in different categories of employment ensuring an effective rollout of welfare measures based on the employment categories. The economic activities of the backward classes and Adivasis were encouraged; markets were set up by the government to ensure fair trade. The government also opened up the economy to entrepreneurs to invest and set up industries in the state. In the backdrop of these impressive initiatives, CM Rajendra Narayan was famously quoted as saying, 'We have a long way to go, but we are on the right path.'

---

[148]The ashram schools were residential middle-schools set up in the tribal areas of the state. The purpose was to provide an all-round education to the tribal children with emphasis on vocational training.

COLLAPSE OF THE COALITION

Despite the Orissa coalition government's impressive record in the first two years, discontentment had begun to brew from within. The inner contradictions between the coalition partners had surfaced. While the Swatantra Party made every effort to keep the coalition alive in the interest of the state, coalition politics did not allow it.

The coalition partner, Mahatab, had begun to lose influence over his party men and the state affairs. He attempted to mitigate this by persuading PM Indira Gandhi to establish a coalition with the Orissa Jana Congress this time, doing away with the Swatantra Party to form a new government in Orissa. He reasoned that, strategically, the Congress would make a good ally owing to its growing popularity in the wake of bank nationalization, the abolition of privy purses and the freedom movement of East Pakistan. Some Orissa Jana Congress leaders were apprehensive of going back to support the Congress.

Indira Gandhi had won the mandate in the 1967 general election and matured as a national leader after taking charge as PM. However, she was facing hurdles in political decision-making from the old guard of the Congress, also known as the Syndicate, and an ideological divide threatened to split the Congress. Eventually, Indira Gandhi and other younger leaders split from the INC in November 1969 to form a rival political organization, which came to be known as Congress (R).

Another threat to the coalition loomed with the impending reports of the commissions of enquiry under Justice Hans Raj Khanna and Justice Janardan Raghunath Mudholkar. In apprehension of the verdict against its own leaders, the Orissa Jana Congress—within two years of forming a government with the Swatantra Party—seemed to have committed itself to withdraw support to gain political relevance. Political relevance will often trump every other motive in any state or nation; the impressive performance of the coalition government in the state did little to sway the decision of the coalition leaders to defect from the government.

The breaking point came when the contents of the Mudholkar Committee leaked out into the public domain. The report allegedly exonerated everyone except Mahatab, which explained why the Orissa Jana Congress wanted to withdraw prematurely and possibly merge with Indira's Congress. They had read the tea leaves. The Mudholkar Committee submitted its report on 29 September 1968. The rumours were true. Mahatab, facing political devastation, challenged the report in court. To protect itself from the scrutiny of central investigative agencies under the PM, the Orissa Jana Congress was attempting to save face by merging with the Congress.[149] The merger did not happen.

A few months later, the media in Delhi got wind of the contents of the Khanna Commission Report. The report, officially revealed on 15 January 1969, instead of incriminating him, gave Biju credit for the great economic prosperity of Orissa during his chief ministership and lauded him for the construction of the Paradip Port, a landmark achievement in the history of Orissa. The only charge the commission found valid was administrative impropriety. It was a reasonable charge and perceived as unavoidable while hastening the progress of the state. This exonerated the former CM and improved his public image. In the midst of thundering applause, Biju Patnaik declared in a public meeting in Cuttack that he would commit a thousand such improprieties in the interest of Orissa's development. His popularity began rising again.

On 31 December 1970, leaders of the Orissa Jana

---

[149]The Orissa Jana Congress eventually merged with the Janata Party in 1977.

Congress—Pabitra Mohan Pradhan, Banamali Patnaik, Prafulla Ghadei, Santanu Das, Upendra Mohanty, Muralidhar Kanungo and Sridhara Das—held a conclave at the residence of the revenue minister, S.N. Patnaik, to take the formal decision to withdraw from the coalition.

AN HONOURABLE EXIT

The government could have survived had it delved into horse-trading, but the erstwhile Maharaja did not allow it. Horse-trading, today, is an inescapable political reality in India, but for Rajendra, it was beneath him. It was a belief he held onto without regret. The CM, realizing the reality of numbers at the floor of the House, tendered his resignation to the governor. It was a decision made out of pure integrity—he had neither lost a no-confidence motion, nor the support of the people. The 46-month government had managed key achievements. The former Maharaja carried an untarnished image of incorruptibility. Red-tapism had been curtailed. Corruption in high places had begun to disappear. The judiciary was successfully separated from the executive. Land revenue was abolished and the administrative machinery was overhauled. The government had also established irrigation projects and reduced taxation on water. The state witnessed a more streamlined panchayati raj system. Key legislations, such as the law against forcible conversion, were passed. The objectives of the Fourth Five-Year Plan however, could not be achieved for lack of resources and the pace of development slowed down because of the none-too-happy Centre—state relations, an issue that still exists today between states that are not politically aligned with the party ruling at the Centre.

The Swatantra Party entered with honour and exited with honour. The stage was set for midterm polls.

11

A Play of Politics

The midterm polls were conducted in an environment of extreme political instability in Orissa alongside the fifth general election to the Lok Sabha in March 1971. In the fray were nine political parties besides Independents that divided the vote in Orissa state. Even Biju, due to his differences with the Congress high command, had formed a breakaway group with his own supporters in 1969, to set up a regional political party in Orissa called the Utkal Congress, which was one of the multiple parties in the line-up for the Assembly seats.

Rajendra Narayan was unable to engage himself in the election campaign with the same energy and enthusiasm of the past years. His strength was waning. The Swatantra Party that bagged 36 seats did not do well in the polls. The Congress (R), led by Nandini Satpathy in Orissa, bagged 51 seats, riding the crest of the Indira wave , while Utkal Congress managed 33 seats. Other parties, like Congress (O) and Orissa Jana Congress secured one seat each, while CPI, PSP, Jharkhand Party and Independents each took away four seats. The bastions of the Swatantra Party, Balangir and Kalahandi, remained intact. However, while the Swatantra Party drew a blank in Dhenkanal, Keonjhar and Balasore, the Utkal Congress failed in Sambalpur, Sundargarh and Phulbani. It was a hung Assembly. No party won the majority.

A SHAKY ALLIANCE

There was an attempt to form a coalition between Congress (R) and the Utkal Congress, but Biju did not trust either Mahatab or Nandini Satpathy. Even Indira Gandhi did not favour a coalition under Mahatab. She preferred Nandini under whose leadership the midterm poll of 1971 was fought and won. As power talks between the parties continued, Biju went on, what he called, a Sadbhavana Yatra or goodwill tour throughout Orissa, in order to avoid pressure from the Congress for entering an alliance.

By the time his Sadbhavana Yatra reached Balangir, Biju was forced to return to Bhubaneshwar as there was a rumour that Swatantra Party was going to form a government with the Utkal Congress. The news surprised many, for it was Rajendra Narayan's government that had initially instituted the Khanna Commission against Biju, but went to change its stance later. Both Biju and Rajendra Narayan, who were charismatic, belonged to a different grade of politicians. They never failed to see the bigger picture and each was outstandingly courageous as individuals. Both possessed a spine of stainless steel and similar magnetism. They decided to come together to form a coalition with Jharkhand Party headed by Biswanath Das that brought in four MLAs. Together they made the majority with 73 seats in a House of 140. The next question was: who would be the CM?

Three names came up for consideration—Biswanath Das, who contested and subsequently won from Rourkela constituency, and two others. Biswanath Das, 82, was the compromise candidate to head the Cabinet. This United Front government under Das was sworn in on 3 April 1971, but remained in office for 14 months only.

Rajendra Narayan became minister, industries and political services. He began with the unfinished agenda of the previous government. Although his health had begun to deteriorate, he did his best to implement the 18-point programme he himself had drafted for the United Front government and continued to take important political decisions on behalf of the government. He was, however, unable to keep usual personal contact with the MLAs of the party, which eventually led to a fallout. A cyclone, too, hit coastal Orissa around this time that slowed the pace of development and destabilized the government.

Once again, there were inherent contradictions among the coalition partners, but the coalition, with a strong instinct for survival had learned from past mistakes and stayed together. However, Das was unable to hold the Cabinet together for long and it was only a matter of time before the government would fall like a pack of cards.

DRAMA IN THE TWILIGHT

Political strategists in the state led by Banka Bihari Das of the Congress had drawn up a neat scheme for a first-rate political crisis. Secret backroom deals had begun and defections were looming. The rebels from the Swatantra Party and the Utkal Congress had secretly decided to withdraw support. So, at a time when the coalition bigwigs from the Utkal Congress and the the Swatantra Party were engaged with private chores, the CM was busy with his granddaughter's wedding, Biju was visiting his constituency in Rajnagar and the Swatantra Party leaders were off attending their party congress in Keonjhar. This was when the rebels struck.[150]

Significant state-level leaders in the Opposition, who were on a visit to the capital, were alerted by a long-distance trunk call from Bhubaneswar. Both Binayak Acharya, leader of opposition, and Braja Mohan Mohanty, the state Congress chief, cut short their Delhi programme and rushed back to Orissa to play their part in the drama about to unfold. The Utkal Congress leader, Nilamani Routray, who only a few days ago had assured Rajendra Narayan that there was no threat to the coalition, suddenly became unavailable. Routray, a close aide of Biju Patnaik, had deserted him and supported the Congress who, it is believed, sought his support with the promise of the post of CM.

In the twilight on 5 June 1972, two cars with eight Swatantra Party and Utkal Congress 'rebels' sped into Raj Bhavan. Forest Minister Gangadhar Pradhan and deputy minister Dambaru Majhi and six other legislators stepped out of the cars to meet the acting governor, Sardar Jogendra Singh, who was expecting them. They handed over a letter stating their desire to withdraw support to the United Front coalition government.

The acting governor asked whether they wrote the petition in question, to which they responded with a yes. On being questioned whether they would retract, they confirmed they wouldn't.

To be doubly sure, the acting governor asked them to put their signature on a sheet of paper and compared those with the ones on the original petition. With his permission, Braja Mohan Mohanty had arranged for a photographer to keep everything on permanent record.

---

[150]Ghosh, Sunit, 'The Grand Finale', *Hindustan Standard.*

Two houses, one in Bhubaneswar and another in Cuttack, were narrowed down on to keep the defectors in hiding, but later, it was thought wise to send them out of the state. So from the Raj Bhavan, the six legislators drove about 450 km along the sea road to Waltair in Vishakhapatnam, Andhra Pradesh via Berhampur. On the way, they changed their car as it broke down. Then they learned that the Orissa police were on their trail, so the six rebels changed course and proceeded to Tirupati.

Acharya too left for Berhampur about the same time, ostensibly, to see his ailing father-in-law. Only Pradhan stayed in his official residence, while the two deputy ministers, Dambaru Majhi and Rabi Singh Majhi, who defected on 6 June, left for their home district Koraput. Thus the political storm signal was hoisted. Ripples were turning into waves. CM Bishwanath Das was compelled to tender his resignation and the coalition collapsed.

CONGRESS GAINS STRENGTH

The Swatantra–Utkal Congress–Jharkhand Party combine was a short-lived coalition that lasted from 3 April 1971 to 9 June 1972. Following the fall of the coalition government, the Congress (R), which had won 49 seats, added the defectors to its strength and its numbers swelled to a majority of 94 seats on 10 June 1972.[151] The party laid the claim to form the next government.

Nandini Satpathy, minister of state at the Centre, sailed into power at the directive of the PM. Routray was bypassed. Nandini was sworn in as CM on 14 June 1972. Shankar

---

[151]Misra, G., 'Bijayananda Patnaik And Ors. vs President Of India And Ors. on 22 October, 1973', https://bit.ly/3N7qoET. Accessed on 21 March 2022.

Dayal Sharma, AICC president, observed that the Adivasis had returned into the Congress fold. Nandini declared that she had come from the Centre to carry Orissa into the national mainstream. The evening Nandini was sworn in, many predicted that the Swatantra Party will be liquidated. When the press sought Rajendra Narayan's reaction to these predictions, he coolly answered, 'If Swatantra Party is liquidated, that would mean the end of opposition. Will the people tolerate the one-party dictatorship? That is exactly the danger against which we have been warning the country.'

Nandini's administration in the state was a replica of Indira Gandhi at the Centre. Nandini came to be known as the 'Iron Lady' of Orissa. As defections continued, the party's strength went up to 96 seats and Nandini became all-powerful. Ministerial berths were handed out to the defectors. Commenting on this, Rajendra Narayan was appalled at the naked and unashamed manner in which defections were being encouraged. He felt that the unscrupulous formation of a government with the support of such defectors will go down as a black chapter in the history of parliamentary democracy in the country.[152] 'Even at this belated stage, I hope the CM will ask the defectors to resign and seek re-election.'[153] Of course, this was hoping against hope because other political parties remained silent as the drama unfolded. Rajendra Narayan's efforts to adhere to principles had no effect. The defectors were awarded with ministerial berths.

Gangadhar Pradhan, as the minister who had engineered the defections into Congress (R), was rewarded with a Cabinet

[152]Sarangi, Suresh Prasad, 'The Role of R.N. Singh Deo in the State Politics of Odisha in the Pre and Post-Independent Political Scenario: A Critical Study', *Odisha Review*, https://bit.ly/3qiAIzZ. Accessed on 9 March 2022.

[153]As recalled by A.U. Singh Deo.

rank. This patchwork through defection was unprecedented. The majority was artificial. Orissa's political life had become muddy and murky. Seeing the rampant defection made Rajendra Narayan 'sadder and wiser'. As rightly said by the famous American essayist, E.P. Whipple, 'A politician weakly and amiably in the right is no match for a politician tenaciously and pugnaciously in the wrong.'[154]

CONTROVERSIAL LAND REFORM

To make matters worse, Nandini was on a mission. On 16 June 1972, within 48 hours of assumption of office as CM, it was rumoured that Nandini was going to promulgate an ordinance bypassing the Assembly, that would ban the mortgage of land by owners of more than 10 acres of area. The proposed ordinance sought to amend the Orissa Land Reform Act of 1960 that provided that no one would be allowed to keep more than 25 standard acres of land for personal cultivation.

Alarmed that principles of democracy were going to be flouted, Rajendra Narayan as the leader of the Opposition wrote to Nandini on 17 June 1972 pointing out that such a measure was neither emergent nor non-controversial enough to warrant an ordinance. He said:

> There is a strong rumour that your government is contemplating to promulgate some ordinance, making important and far-reaching amendment in the Land Reform Act. The Constitution provides for promulgation of ordinance when the Assembly is not in session only to meet situations of emergency. Even then ordinances

[154]Marden, Orison Swett, *Architects of Fate - Or, Steps to Success and Power: A Book Designed to Inspire Youth to Character Building, Self- Culture and Noble Achievement,* Read Books, 2019.

> may be justified only on non-controversial matters. I hope your government will not commit any impropriety of promulgating ordinances on important and controversial matters and will give the Assembly the opportunity of fullest debate and discussion before the proposed legislation is enacted into law.[155]

For Rajendra Narayan, it meant a gross misuse of ordinance-making power. The government did not see reason and the ordinance was promulgated. The ordinance was ill-conceived and ill-considered to project an image of progressivism and radicalism. It instead created instability, insecurity and confusion.

In February 1973, Nandini introduced the Land Reform Bill which fixed the ceiling at 10 standard acres. This meant the government would take away surplus land from landowners and redistribute the land—two acres each—among the poor. The objective of the government was to acquire surplus land and redistribute it among the landless to improve the economy and living standards of the weaker sections of society. It would wreak havoc among the landowners in the state. Rajendra Narayan could assess the ramifications of the Bill and vociferously opposed it.

The government labelled his stand as conservative and feudalistic because large acres of land were only available with the erstwhile maharajas. Land reform was an issue that Nehru had originally spearheaded after being surprised at the scale of land owned by Babu Lal Chand, one of the wealthiest zamindars of North Bihar.[156] It was a contentious issue. Owing to his vested interest, one may not agree with Rajendra Narayan, but the facts and arguments he advanced

---

[155]R.N. Singh Deo, private letter to Nandini Satpathy, 17 June 1972.

[156]Singh, N.K., *Portraits of Power: Half a Century of Being at Ringside,* Rupa Publications, 2020.

to advocate this cause were so convincing and persuasive that a reader, free from political prejudices, would be compelled to agree. Rajendra Narayan opined that there was no ostensible reason or scientific basis for the fixation of a ceiling at 10 standard acres. In fact, it was known that the smaller the land, the lesser the yield.

He recalled, 'Nehru had promised that land reform would not be tampered with for at least 15 years after Independence. Later, the original Act of 1960 brought down the ceiling from 33 acres to 25 acres. Subsequent amendments until 1970 stipulated a land ceiling of 20 standard acres. Why isn't this ceiling being implemented? Why is the ceiling being further reduced to 10 acres in Orissa?'[157] Other states had a higher land ceiling. In Rajasthan, it was 150–170 acres, while Andhra Pradesh, Haryana, Punjab, Maharashtra and Madhya Pradesh, etc., which were Congress states, had fixed the land ceiling at 18 standard acres. Why was the directive different for Orissa?

Rajendra Narayan was of the view that reduction of land ceiling would hurt the marginal farmers. He even quoted the then current Economic Survey Report, which stated that less than 15 acres will affect productivity and mean the annihilation of the farm economy. He therefore argued: 'There is no justification for reduction of production for decentralization of land. A farmer needs minimum six acres of land to maintain one plough unit. To be cost-efficient, a single tractor must cultivate one thousand acres.'[158]

Revenue Minister S.N. Patnaik's statement on the radio that individual ownership of land must go in order to increase

---

[157]Discussion on the floor of the Assembly, Orissa Land Reforms Amendment Bill, 17 February 1973. Orissa Assembly Archives.

[158]Ibid.

productivity worried Rajendra Narayan. He opined, 'This is hidden communism. The aim is to take away individual ownership and impose social ownership, which has not worked in China that declared state ownership of land. Everyone in China became a servant, with neither freedom nor the right to protest. Cultivation happens at the point of the gun.'[159] Rajendra Narayan, like Maharashtra's former agriculture minister, believed that the basis for land reform should be increase in productivity and establishment of the right of the farmer like in cooperative farming because surplus land would never be adequate for distribution.

Biju later observed, 'The arguments advanced by Rajendra Narayan smack of Swatantra ideology, of Indian conservatism. We may not agree, but that is not necessary in a democracy. We, however, have to admit that he was well-informed and his logic is irrefutable. When PSP merged with the Congress, he said, it was all right but the party should not sell its soul to communism, or, to the Congress.'

Rajendra Narayan had strong opinions that were based on reason. He said nothing to play to the gallery. He did nothing for populism or opportunism. He did not oppose for the sake of opposition or to gain political mileage. He also found public support from Ram Manohar Lohia on this issue.

PROMOTING ACCOUNTABILITY

As leader of the opposition, he did his utmost to ensure that democracy worked for the people and he was never afraid to speak up. In July 1972, in view of the price rise, he requested Nandini to raise the minimum wages from ₹1 to ₹3 a day through an ordinance before the silver jubilee celebration of

---

[159]Ibid.

India's independence. In the letter, he mentioned that unless some positive relief is given to the weaker sections immediately, the fanfare around the celebration of our national independence will be a cruel irony to these people. The government wasn't interested in prudent advice!

Nandini's government did not carry much public popularity in terms of performance. Their attempts at diminishing their rivals did not help the matter. The administration had totally become stagnant. Files were getting piled up. Rajendra Narayan commented, 'Raising false hopes through false promises, these Congress ministers have learnt one thing from Dr Goebbels, that the greater the untruth, the more prone are the people to believe it.' Nandini Satpathy had brought in a government which did not seem to fully understand how Odias thought and functioned. The authoritarian manner with which she executed her policies irked both her political rivals as well as the poorest sections of the voters.

Rajendra Narayan worked to expose the doublespeak of the government. He was unsparing in exposing the manoeuvres and machinations behind Nandini's poll victory in the Cuttack by-elections, the manipulation of voters' list, misuse of government vehicles and government officers, etc., which constituted a flagrant violation of the model code of conduct, unprecedented in the political history of Orissa. Naturally, this state of affairs wouldn't last long.

A NEW UNITED FRONT

Orissa faced an unprecedented political crisis. Nandini's ministry was, in fact, a patch-up of six different factions, each pulling in six different directions. So there was continuous tension. The mass exodus from Utkal Congress and the defection from the Swatantra Party was not an asset for the

Congress. There were many queuing up for power. Congress had slammed its door on Biju. A sizeable section of the Congress had revolted against the 'progressive' land reform measure and some against nationalization of kendu leaf trade. Dissidents exerted pressure. There was a factional feud. Many clamoured for a change of leadership. 'Nandini must go' had become a refrain. There was a signature campaign against her.

Defections became the norm in the state. Never before had the prestige of the legislative Assembly been in so much disrepute. Orissa's political climate had become murky. Both Mahatab and Biju, even though they were heading regional parties, found themselves isolated and sought Rajendra Narayan's help. They agreed that constituting a strong, viable opposition to pre-empt further defections to the ruling party was a democratic necessity. Mahatab, Biju and Rajendra Narayan contemplated an alliance. Rajendra Narayan wrote to the Swatantra Party's central leadership for advice.

A move was initiated among Swatantra Party, Utkal Congress and independent groups to once again pool in their strength together. They accepted that only a united party could pose a challenge to the Congress. While the correspondence continued, a telegram from Madhu Mehta, general secretary of the Swatantra Party, was leaked out into the press. The telegram which asked Rajendra Narayan not to align with Biju or Mahatab was made public on the behest of Nandini Satpathy. Even as the showdowns continued, Rajendra Narayan requested the central leadership of the Swatantra Party for approval of this new combine in the name of the Pragati Legislature Party (PLP). This new party—a three-party alliance of the Opposition parties—was formed in January 1973 and consisted of 48 members—25 from the Swatantra Party,

18 from the Utkal Congress and five from Mahatab's party.[160] Under Biju's leadership, the party streamlined its common programme of action and agreed to function jointly in the legislative Assembly.

KENDU LEAF VENDETTA

Riled by the political happenings, the regime instituted an enquiry commission against Rajendra Narayan. G.K. Mitter, a retired judge of the Supreme Court, constituted the one-man commission to institute an investigation into the 'shady kendu leaf deal'[161] of 1970 and 1971, wherein the state government had given concessions to contractors and renewed their contract before time, without holding any public auction or calling for fresh tenders.

It is significant that the terms of reference for the Mitter Commission were to exclusively probe into the rebate and renewal of government order on kendu leaf trade. When the rebate order was issued in 1970, Rajendra Narayan was the CM and H.P. Mohapatra was the forest minister, both being from the Swatantra Party. On 23 September 1971, when the contract of the existing leaseholders was renewed, Biswanath Das was the CM and Ainthu Sahu was the forest minister. However, Das was not made a party to this. To this day, leading politicians of Orissa on all sides maintain that the purpose of the commission seemed politically motivated instead of being a genuine probe into corruption.

As a contrast to this, Rajendra Narayan, when he was the

---

[160]Pattanaik, Tusar Kanta, 'The role of the CM of Orissa a case study of Biju Patnaik', Department of Political Science, Utkal University, 2003.

[161]Kendu or tendu leaves are used for wrapping bidis, a popular smoke among the poor, and constitute one of the most important non-wood forest products of Orissa.

CM, had appointed the Khanna Commission to probe into acts of corruption by Congress ministers; it was set up for fact-finding and not witch-hunting. He believed in political ethics and that those who transgressed must be brought to book, however high or mighty. He was never vindictive and even forgave his political adversaries. Moreover, once he had appointed the commissions, his job was done. He neither interfered nor attempted to influence the judgment. In fact, the Khanna Commission which seemed to be against Biju Patnaik, ultimately gave him a certificate that helped him. Even Biju did not misunderstand Rajendra Narayan on this count, and his respect and regard for him endured until the end.

It is true that kendu leaf traders are known to contribute substantially to the finances of the ruling party in the state every year. Even the Mudholkar Commission that ruled against Mahatab, had described the kendu leaf contracts as the 'bane of Orissa politics'. The Mudholkar Commission bears testimony to the nexus between powerful politicians, the kendu leaf contractors and mine-owners for political purposes. Several Orissa politicians' names had been linked to the powerful kendu leaf cartel.

Possibly, even the Orissa branch of the Swatantra Party led by the Rajendra Narayan was running short of funds. Unlike the Congress, backed by the industrial magnates and known to be the richest party at the time, the rise and fall of governments caused by frequent floor-crossings by MLAs, leading to midterm polls had eaten into the slender purse of the party, made leaner with the short supply from the central Swatantra Party. With increasing election expenses, it was difficult to run the party. The privy purse on which Rajendra Narayan had supported the Parishad was abolished, following Indira Gandhi's deviation from the late Vallabhbhai's promise.

Rajendra Narayan had mentioned in his affidavit placed before the Mitter Commission: rationalization of fixed rates for the kendu leaf traders was chiefly to curb smuggling. It was part of the Swatantra Party ideology and party philosophy: the lower the taxation, higher the production. The annual lease extended for a three-year term in 1970 was another bone of contention. To this charge, Rajendra Narayan responded that the delay in giving approval would have helped continue corrupt practices, resulting in loss of income to the state. Moreover, as the season was ending, the contractors could have declined to take up the lease on account of delay by the government that would have then been forced to lease it out to substitute contractors at 'throw-away cost'.

The Mitter Commission submitted its report in August 1974,[162] long after the Nandini government had an ignominious exit. Still, the situation had given Nandini a handle to work with and she made full capital out of it. Even though Rajendra Narayan was clean and unafraid, he knew Nandini was determined to take him out of politics given that he was a powerful political rival. Rajendra Narayan knew where his rivals would strike. If his unblemished image was tarnished, he would be kept out of the way, there would be no opposition in Orissa, and where a veteran politician like Mahatab had failed, Satpathy would succeed. However, the Nandini government could not overshadow the goodwill Rajendra Narayan had worked all his life to create. He stood apart from his ilk as a politician with a difference and went on to win the next election. His popular support remained unaffected even as Nandini's government went on to confront its existential crisis.

---

[162]Mitter, G.K., 'Report of the Commission of Enquiry', Government of Orissa, 1974.

KARMA AT WORK

Twenty-five Congress MLAs suddenly walked out of the ruling Congress and demanded seats for a separate group. Rajendra Narayan knew that a tide is always followed by an ebb. Nandini, who had sown winds, now reaped whirlwinds. Following these defections, her ministry collapsed, only eight months after taking charge. The end came before sunset, the same day when Nandini resigned and advised the Governor B.D. Jatti to dissolve the assembly. By doing this, she forestalled the government's defeat on the floor of the House and the coming of the Pragati Party to power. The Congress turncoats returned to the Utkal Congress, which had with Mahatab already become part of the PLP alongside Rajendra Narayan. The same evening, Banka Bihari Das hinted at the institution of yet another enquiry commission against allegations of corruption regarding kendu leaf trade in the previous two ministries. It was obviously directed against Rajendra Narayan as a warning to either withdraw from the combine or face commission.

Two days later, *The Hindu* carried a report on Nandini's government. It read:[163]

> None will refuse Ms Satpathy's charge that the politics of Orissa has been vitiated by rampant corruption and administrative impropriety. But she would have been on better ground to combat it and to give a more wholesome turn to Orissa politics if she had not ridden to power on the crest of induced opportunistic defections and also sought to maintain it somehow without much regard to democratic proprieties... The most stable and purposeful regime that Orissa enjoyed in recent years was perhaps

---

[163]'Ms Nandini Satpathy's Exit', *The Hindu,* 3 March 1973.

> that of the coalition led by Swatantra Party leader, Mr Rajendra Narayan. Its downfall was contrived by the Congress. The biter has been bit, but backward Orissa's pressing problems may have to wait, while the interminable politicking goes on.

Orissa was once again ready to go to the polls to seek a fresh mandate. The Nandini government lasted only 263 days. Biju Patnaik put up his claim to form the government. Governor Jatti knew that PLP could form a stable ministry, but did not accept Biju's claim. Orissa came under president's rule on 3 March 1973 for the third time after independence. Biju appealed to the high court. But it rejected the writ on the ground that the petition was not within its purview. It, however, opined that the governor should have invited the leader of the PLP to form the government as per the convention.

Meanwhile, in a reorganization of constituencies, the number of seats in Orissa Assembly was increased to 147.[164] The next midterm poll was held on 22 February 1974. The Congress and CPI fought the election together. Utkal Congress, Swatantra Party and the United Socialist Party of Ram Manohar Lohia united and fought under PLP on an 11-point common programme. The polls saw a major victory for Rajendra Narayan and the Swatantra Party that bagged nine Assembly seats and parliament seat of Balangir district to the utter discomfiture of the Congress (R) leadership in Orissa. The Congress, riding on the Indira wave of 'Garibi Hatao', won 69 seats, Utkal Congress won 35, Swatantra Party snapped up 21 seats, the CPI got seven seats, United Socialist Party

[164]Verma, A.K., 'Fourth Delimitation of Constituencies: An Appraisal', *Economic and Political Weekly*, 15 March 2008, https://bit.ly/36xYr8q. Accessed on 21 March 2022.

(USP) managed two, CPI (M) won three seats while Orissa Jana Congress managed a single seat only. Independents won eight out of 147 seats. Congress became the single majority party. With CPI's support, its number soared to 76 while the PLP got 57.[165]

The Swatantra Party, the Utkal Congress and the USP, which had formed the 'Pragati Dal'[166], merged into Charan Singh's Bharatiya Lok Dal to enable a real chance at becoming a national party. The Bharatiya Kranti Dal, Rashtriya Loktantrik Dal, Kisan Mazdur Party followed suit. Rajendra Narayan became a member of the executive committee of the Bharatiya Lok Dal.

Nandini Satpathy formed the government for the second time on 6 March 1974. She reigned uninterrupted till the Emergency that unleashed a tidal wave of political tension setting the stage for Jaya Prakash Narayan's Sampurna Kranti.

---

[165]*Statistical Report on General Election, 1974, to The Legislative Assembly of Orissa*, Election Commission of India, New Delhi.

[166]Another name for the Orissa Pragati Legislature Party.

12

Back to Balangir

vasamsi jirnani yatha vihaya
navani grhnati naro 'parani
tatha sarirani vihaya jirnany
anyani samyati navani dehi[167]

[As a person puts on new garments,
giving up old ones, similarly,
the soul accepts new material bodies,
giving up the old and useless ones.]

Rajendra Narayan was a conscientious leader with a dexterous work ethic. He was a hands-on leader and when he worked, he maintained no schedule, often forgetting to eat. Although his unceasing efforts left a legacy, which would be remembered and envied several generations after his time, overworking had impaired his health seriously. The powers and temptations that came along with the titles—His Royal Highness and CM—never got to his head. It was

[167]Chapter 2, Verse 22, Bhagavad Gita.

this very quality that truly made him the people's king.

Towards the end of his life, the thirtieth and last ruling maharaja of the princely state of Patna was left ill and weak. He was suffering from spondylitis. There was a hushed rumour that he had become seriously ill on account of smoking. Rajendra Narayan was being treated by Dr Sarat Chandra Mishra, an eminent physician of Cuttack. But none, however close, knew what exact ailment he was suffering from. The former Maharaja knew he was dying, but did not disclose it.

His health deteriorated before the budget session of February 1975. He was taken to North Avenue, New Delhi, where his son, Raj Raj Singh Deo, also an MP, was staying. A quick check-up was scheduled at AIIMS after which he was meant to return to Bhubaneswar and then to his constituency to his people. The Maharani, Kailash Kumari, was then to proceed to Sri Lanka to attend a satsang to be addressed by Sri Sri Sri Shivabalayogi Maharaj, their guru.

A short while after he arrived at Raj Raj's house, he was rushed to Mumbai to the Tata Cancer Institute in Bombay. Rajendra Narayan had successfully concealed his ailment till so long. On 20 February 1975, he was visited by close friends, which included H.H. Maharaja Pratap Kesari Deo of Kalahandi and Loknath Misra, then MP from Rajya Sabha. They discussed the volatile political atmosphere in the country, which would later snowball into the infamous Emergency period.

On hearing about the rapidly deteriorating condition of the Maharaja, his family began to arrive in Bombay. He was particularly pleased to see his sisters. In sickness and in health, there was no dearth of loyal supporters, loved ones and followers who came to pay their respects to what no one knew was to be his final days. On 22 February 1975, he instructed his eldest son Raj Raj to send a letter to their guru Sri Shivabalayogi Maharaj, informing him that the former

Maharaja was prepared to be relieved of his pain and suffering. That very evening, he breathed his last. The news of his passing away spread like wildfire across the country.

Most in Orissa heard of his ailment only after the news of his passing away. All national flags in the state flew at half-mast in mourning. Shops and schools were shut down and offices were closed. Both the governments of Orissa and Maharashtra pledged to make arrangements for his mortal remains to be flown to Orissa for the final rites, as per the Maharaja's last wishes. However, neither government managed to successfully make these arrangements in time. His younger son, Ananga Uday, eventually hired a private aircraft to transport the family and the Maharaja's remains back to Bhubaneswar.

The state government presented a guard of honour and his remains were then transported to Balangir, the erstwhile capital of Patna State. Thousands of people gathered at the airport for a glimpse of their leader's last journey. They were lined up on both sides of the road to see the funeral procession proceed from Bhubaneswar to Balangir. The bereaved crowd cried, '*Rajendra Narayan amar rahe!* [Long live Rajendra Narayan]' as their voices echoed in the distance. The funeral procession was so overwhelmed by crowds that it took many hours to arrive in Balangir as it had to stop several times so that the local villagers and citizens could pay their last respects to their departed leader. All the arrangements were personally supervised by Biju, then leader of opposition.

The Maharaja was a tall figure in Orissa, his legacy and loss was deeply felt. The hero's welcome his remains received on his last journey to Balangir is testament to his service for his people. As long as he was politically active, the Congress and opposition never succeeded in making significant inroads into Orissa.

Even though it is widely believed among political circles today that the state and the administration over the years following his passing away did not show an appropriate respect for his legacy, his work, however, far overshadows any administrative ceremonies or homages made in his memory.

The erstwhile king of Balangir and CM is remembered far more fondly for his Gandhian principles of 'simple living and high thinking', his ability to remain calm and composed even in the darkest of times and his extraordinary compassion towards the poor and downtrodden whom he would regularly visit. In a sense, Orissa's politics and administration was given a modern identity, ironically by a monarch rising from a pre-democratic era. He will forever remain immortal in the memories of thousands of Odias he helped uplift from the dark ages of oppression and superstition. As many of them proudly state, 'We lived in his time,' which is an identity far more eternal than any worldly titles.

13

Man and Statesman

India's history is filled with pioneers, artists, statesmen and visionaries. The giants among men, who are remembered not for their lifestyle or pedigree but their selfless service for humanity, are rare. Rajendra Narayan Singh Deo was a true king among kings. His intolerance for autocracy and brilliant intellect combined to create an enviable legacy among the royal houses of princely India. He was not only a level-headed politician, but every inch a true gentleman. He was called Maharaja in popular parlance, a rare respect given by the people in independent, democratic India. Some ministers would even forward files with handwritten notes saying, 'Maharaja may decide.'

He was not fond of this nomenclature, not because it reminded him of the state he had lost, or the irrecoverable position gone, but more so because he was no longer the Maharaja. On one occasion when someone called him Maharaja, he playfully remarked, 'I'm no longer a maharaja. Patel took away my state, Indira, the privy purse. And what remains now? We are common citizens like you.'[168] It was said with a smile and he meant it.

He was Gandhian in thought and deed. While on an election campaign, he would not hesitate to ride a bicycle or lie down to rest on the veranda of a launderer or satisfy his hunger with handfuls of puffed rice in a hut. Given his power and plenitude, his titles and positions, his ordinariness was rather strange. Maharaja Bhupinder Singh, his father-in-law, once said, 'I was born a Maharaja, I can only behave as one. I would look false and phoney if I tried to be someone else.' Rajendra Narayan knew he was not born a maharaja. The power and position of monarchy and head of state was thrust upon him.

READY TO SERVE

In January 1935, a year after the Bihar earthquake, Rajendra Narayan suddenly disappeared from Calcutta where he was staying. Only the Maharani knew of his whereabouts. It was later discovered that he was involved in volunteer work and even assisted the victims of the Quetta Earthquake in 1935 in a simple khaddar uniform.[169] When Gandhi was assassinated, Rajendra Narayan was the only raja from Orissa who walked behind the funeral cortège of the Mahatma from Birla Bhawan to Rajghat on 31 January 1948. When Khan Abdul Gaffar Khan, or 'Frontier Gandhi', as he was lovingly known, visited Orissa, Rajendra Narayan received him at Rourkela airstrip, carried his bag to the car and made him the state guest. It was a rare sight for the people who had gathered there to see the CM and former maharaja of a princely state carrying the

---

[168]From a conversation to which A.U. Singh Deo was a witness.

[169]As retold by the Late Maharani Kailash Kumari of Patna.

personal belongings of the great warrior from Afghanistan. It was, of course, quite natural for one, who had the highest regard for Gandhi and his ideals, to do so.

In 1968, as CM, he had introduced a law against forcible religious conversion. This law sent tremors throughout the country. Christian delegations came to hear from him. He explained to them that it was a general order applicable to all conversions from Hinduism to Islam, from Christianity to Hinduism, etc. There is no place for force in religion. His Independence Day speech after being sworn in as CM demonstrates his deep engagement and concern for the people for whom he felt deep responsibility:

> Commemoration of national events of importance like the Independence Day provide us the occasion to look back into the past and look ahead into the future. For historical reasons, we, in Orissa, had lagged behind some other states at the dawn of independence and, unless this disparity in development disappears, we would continue to be a backward state despite our rich natural and human resources. We have been persistently pleading with the Government of India for removal of this regional imbalance. Time will dictate the necessity for development, especially for those who have been left behind on the path to India's growth and prosperity with no hope. All that is required of us is to be conscious about it and not to slacken our efforts to secure this desirable and necessary objective.
>
> Improving the lot of the common man is one of the primary objectives of our government. The time-honoured profession of agriculture, with which most of our people are occupied, is only at subsistence level. Apart from revolutionizing agriculture with the scientific knowledge

> and inputs now available for higher production in those areas where irrigation facilities exist, we have also a number of schemes and programmes, which are being implemented, designed to improve the economic condition of the farmers. These schemes are employment-oriented with a bias toward production.
>
> We have also been consistently trying to mitigate the hardship of the educated unemployed. A number of nationalized and other commercial banks have offered loan facilities or self-employment to assist the educated unemployed including medical and engineering graduates.
>
> The days ahead of us are difficult and would require the sustained cooperation, goodwill, sacrifice, discipline, hard work and devotion to duty for all. Let us enter into the twenty-fourth year of Independence with these thoughts in mind, so that, united we may take the state forward.[170]

It is common for politicians to become students of a powerful spiritual guru, a preceptor for divine protection. P.V. Narasimha Rao had Acharya Chandraswami, while Nandini Satapathy followed Mirra Alfassa in the Sri Aurobindo Ashram. Rajendra Narayan was a student of Sri Shivabalayogi Maharaj, an enlightened master who has been a guide to the entire family. Rajendra Narayan used to devote an hour a day to yoga, meditation, pranayama and Chandi Path.[171] He had read the Bhrigu Samhita, Tibetan tantra of Lama Taranath and wore an *ek mukhi* or single faced rudraksha and had a naga image on his neck.

---

[170]Speech of the CM of Odisha, 15 August 1967, Odisha State Archives, Bhubaneswar.

[171]Chandi Path, a sacred text containing 700 verses, is part of the Markandeya Purana. It's recitation helps one concentrate on the presence of Chandi, the Divine Mother, so that the conflicted mind may return to peace.

A PATRON OF CULTURE

In post-Independence India, Rajendra Narayan played an important role in shaping the political destiny of the state and strengthening the democratic structure of Indian polity. A statesman and a parliamentarian of no mean order, his modesty, astute administrative acumen, passion for work, political discipline, diplomatic wisdom and personal charm earned him the affection and admiration of many, including those of other political and ideological persuasions.

As the ruler of Patna State, he established the fully-equipped Koshal Kalamandal, Balangir, which was a cultural centre of vocal and instrumental music, dance and drama. The Kalamandal, set up with a fixed deposit of ₹32 lakh in the Kolkata City Bank, not only encouraged the talent of young artists, it also published a weekly newspaper, *Patna Dipika*, on the lines of *Utkal Dipika*, the first Odia newspaper and a monthly literary journal, *Chaturanga*, at a time when such journals were shutting down in Orissa for lack of patronage.

Patna Dipika carried advertisements, court notices, market prices besides literary essays. On 28 February 1946, when *Patna Dipika* brought out its second issue, Rajendra Narayan personally donated ₹15,000 and assured them pay of ₹5,000 every month. *Patna Dipika's* first editor was his own brother, Brajendra Narayan Singh Deo of Seraikela, and managing editor was Ganga Prasad Panda.

On the editorial board of *Chaturanga* were distinguished men of letters of Orissa like Kalindi Panigrahi, Kabichandra Kalicharan Patnaik, Bidhu Bhusan Guru, Rajyaratna Balabhadra Bohidar, Samuel Naik and Prabhat Mukherjee. Its contributors included eminent writers like Gopinath Mohanty, Naba Kishore Das, Benudhar Rout, Sachidananda Routray, Binod Rautarai, Sashi Bhusan Ray, Surendra Mohanty, Gaurikumar

Brahma, Chintamani Behera, Raj Kishore Roy and Raj Kishore Patnaik. There was one Dalaganjan Press in Balangir, but *Chaturanga* had its own press and during the paper shortage after World War II, it was brought out on handmade paper.

Rajendra Narayan offered his privy purse not only to artists but also to meritorious students pursuing courses like Ayurveda, Veterinary Science, Astrology, Physical Science, etc., and also gave them jobs in his own royal administration on their return. Historian Purna Chandra Rath was given financial support of ₹200 a month from 1945 to 1947, to quote a single example out of so many during the lifetime of a magnanimous patron of culture.

He was also interested in history and heritage. He acquired the *Kosalananda Kavya*, 150 a palm-leaf manuscript, written in Sanskrit in 1664, translated into Odia, which is still preserved in the Odisha State Museum.

In collaboration with Maharaja Pratap Kesari Deo of Kalahandi, Rajendra Narayan started the Kalinga Historical Research Society, which published an all-India historical journal. A museum was also set up by the society; it was one of the first museums in Orissa. The specimens of ancient sculpture, coins, copperplates, etc., were collected from places like Kusanga, Athgan, Saintala, Titlagarh, Ranipur-Jharial, etc. On one of these copper plates was inscribed the rare image of Ardhanarishvara.[172] This museum eventually led to the creation of Odisha State Museum at Bhubaneswar.

He established a Department of Archeology with Purna Chandra Rath, BA, BEd, MRAS (Bengal) as superintendent. Rath was deputed by Rajendra Narayan to visit historical places in the country like Peshawar, Taxila, Amritsar, Delhi, Agra,

---

[172]The ancient depiction of the male and female androgynous form of Shiva and Parvati.

Sarnath, Benares, etc. In 1944–45, the Maharaja sent Rath to Taxila[173] for a three-month archaeological training.

As an administrator, a parliamentarian, an artist, a patron of life and as a patriot, his contributions to post-Independence Orissa were immense. It will come to the surface in due course of time. Men rise and fall standing the test of times, and those who choose to remain on the right side of history are remembered as the true agents of change and progress. The name of the Maharaja Rajendra Narayan Singh Deo will never fade from the consciousness of the state of Orissa.

[173]Taxila is a well-known archaeological site in the modern city by the same name in Punjab, Pakistan.

Epilogue

Rajendra Narayan Singh Deo was born in a large family with eight siblings. On growing up, he headed a joint family, a Garjat, a party and an entire state. He had five brothers and three sisters who were married into royal families. While Ratnaprabha Devi married Raja Shankar Pratap Singh Deo Mahindra Bahadur of Dhenkanal, Hemaprabha Devi became the senior Maharani of Maharajadhiraj Yadavindra Singh of Patiala; Maniprabha Devi became the Rani of Jagannath Rajmani Raj Deo of Manjusha.

His eldest brother Tikayat Nrupendra Narayan Singh Deo of Seraikela was married in Kalahandi and excelled as vice president of the Seraikela State Development Council and member of the Standing Committee of Ministers in the Chamber of Princes between 1934 and 1947. Among the four other brothers, Shuvendhra and Sudhendra Narayan Singh Deo were both accomplished Chhau dancers of international repute; Brajendra Narayan Singh Deo rose to become the zamindar of Jarasingha Estate in Balangir and Bhoopendra Narayan Singh Deo was married in Gondal.

Married to Maharani Kailash Kumari of Patiala, Rajendra Narayan established a large family of his own. He had six children: four daughters and two sons. The Maharaja's daughters were educated at Loreto Convent Intermediate

College, Lucknow. His eldest daughter Rajshree Devi was married to Thakur Prithvirajsinjhi of Sayla, Gujarat. She had one son and one daughter. His second daughter, Brajshree, married Ripudaman Singh, Raja of Bhadawar near Agra. She was blessed with a son and a daughter. While Brajshree's son, Aridaman Singh became a minister in the UP Cabinet, her daughter Rajkumari Madhulika Singh was married to Maharajkumar Shiladitya Singh of Narsingarh.

The Maharaja's third daughter, Roopshree Devi, was married to Ranavijay Shahi, zamindar of Dumaria, Bihar, and had three sons and one daughter. The Maharaja's fourth daughter was Krishna Kumari who was married to Captain Baldev Singh of Jalalpur, Aligarh, and went on to have three sons—Aditya, Abhimanyu and Chandrachur Singh. While Aditya and Abhimanyu are in the TV production business, Chandrachur is a well-known and respected actor in the Hindi film industry.

His oldest son, Raj Raj Singh Deo, was born in 1934 and was sent to Mayo College, Ajmer, the same institution where his father studied as an outstanding scholar. Raj Raj was an MP for a decade. He is survived by two sons, Kanakavardhan and Srivardhan, and two daughters, Mitravinda and Satya Rajeswari. Both Kanakavardhan and his wife Sangita Kumari, who hails from from Rajasthan, are politicians affiliated with the Bharatiya Janata Party. While Kanakavardhan was minister, urban development in Orissa, Sangita is an MP. Raj Raj's younger son, Srivardhan, is married to Prakriti Devi from Jodhpur and has a son and a daughter.

The Maharaja's youngest son is Anang Uday Singh Deo. He was a student at the Doon School, and got married to Vijay Lakshmi Devi of Jagirsar, Balia district, UP. Anang Uday has been elected to the Orissa Assembly six times. He has been a Cabinet Minister, holding different important portfolios, and till recently, was an MP in the Rajya Sabha. Of his three sons, Kalikesh Narayan, Manmath Vijay and Arkesh Narayan, Kalikesh is a former MLA and also a former member of Lok Sabha and a politician with promise. Manmath and Arkesh Singh Deo are successful businessmen and actively involved in the politics of the state.

As the head of a large family, Rajendra Narayan worked to inculcate the values of tolerance, patience, mutual understanding and love that asks for nothing and gives everything. Contrarily, in a nuclear family where one is 'cribbed, cabined and confined', one tends to be self-centred, unsympathetic and non-cooperative, even aggressive.

His work as the head of a large family or even his political party was difficult, but he made it seem easy with his experience and, more importantly, his liberal humanism which was a congenital trait. He was accommodating and affectionate. He cared and shared. As the undisputed leader of the GP and then the Swatantra Party, he used to keep in close contact with his roots. He paid equal attention to those who were on the top echelon and to the nameless, mute members of the party.

As an indefatigable defender of democratic values, he knew there would be dissent but believed that dissent should not lead to dissension. Rajendra Narayan Singh Deo not only tolerated his political rivals, he also lived and worked alongside them in harmony. His goal was the well-being of the people—he never lost track of this vision and worked tirelessly for the welfare of Orissa and, of course, India.

Acknowledgements

Rajendra Narayan Singh Deo was born into a royal family and was the maharaja of a state. Yet, his life had not been appropriately assessed, observed MP Surendra Mohanty ruefully. His culture and refinement, his love for art and literature, dance and music, his large heartedness and gentleness, his firmness and evenhandedness, his fealty to democracy and loyalty to the constitution, his tireless defense of individual liberty and human dignity made him what he was—an ideal ruler, an ideal leader and an ideal man.

He was the maharaja from 1933 to 1947, an MP from 1952 to 1956, leader of opposition, Orissa Assembly, from 1957 to 1959 and then again from 1961 to 1966. He was also deputy CM from 1971 to 1973 and the CM from 1967 to 1971. Thus, he had seen life both from opposition desks and from treasury benches. He had seen it steadily and seen it whole, to borrow a phrase from Matthew Arnold.

It is true, his life was largely political, yet unlike the life of a politician, it was an open book, for he had nothing to exclude and nothing to expose. He was balanced and just. He was honest and sincere. Truthful to men and faithful to God, he had love towards all and malice towards none. He made no promise he could not keep. He handled no power that did not keep him humble. He did not play to the gallery.

He did not pray to his mortal masters for self-aggrandizement and self-advancement. He was frank and he was fair. He said what he meant and meant what he said.

He was more than a politician; he was a statesman, inspired by love for men, love for the country and love for God. He never abandoned his habitual cool in spite of political reverses. He rescued governments and safeguarded even his rivals. He was a dauntless defender of democratic traditions and liberal values, a fearless crusader of civil liberty and constitutional propriety.

He remained a Maharaja his entire life, a name by which he was often called and often recalled by, long after his bones were interred.

I am grateful to Anang Uday Singh Deo, MP, Rajya Sabha, without whose generosity, this work about an illustrious son of India could not have seen the light of day. And, of course, to Prof. G.P. Guru, former director of Mass Education, Orissa, for his valuable suggestions. My thanks are due to all those who have in various ways and in various places lent their hands to make this work what it is. Last but not least, I thank Sarada Nanda who has typed out my version of the manuscript so neatly and ungrudgingly.

—Pabitra Mohan Nayak

Among the titans of leadership who have emerged from the princely states, Maharaja Rajendra Narayan Singh Deo is a symbol of Odia pride and culture that has sustained itself for generations. He entered into electoral politics and fought elections to rise and govern as the CM as gracefully as he had while he was the sovereign ruler.

Real transformation entails honesty of self and one's

purpose; the Maharaja exhibited both these qualities equally. It has been an immense honour and pleasure to research and write about him. I am grateful to Yamini Chowdhury of Rupa Publications for her patience and timely interventions to finish this manuscript. This entire piece with two authors and their own writing styles would not have blended into easy readability without the hours and patience of the Rupa team, whose guidance has made me even better at my writing.

I would like to thank K. Natwar Singh, his wife, Kunwarani Hemendra Kaur, and Maharajkumar Ananga Uday Singh Deo for encouraging me, and entrusting Prof. Nayak and me with this important historical record.

The book would not have been possible without the valuable inputs given by Brig. (Retd) Raja K.P. Singh Deo, Dhenkanal, Rajkumar B.K. Singh Deo, Manjusha, Raja Pratap Aditya Singh Deo, Seraikela, Kunwarani Krishna Singh, Jalalpur, Kunwar Sanjay Singh Badnor, Rani Madhulika Kumari, Narsinghar, and Ajaya Kumar Das.

—V.R. Singh

Bibliography

NEWSPAPERS, PERIODICALS, PAMPHLETS AND GAZETTEERS

'The Koshal Tract, Balangir': Koshal Sangha, Calcutta, Thackers Press and Dictionaries, n.d.

Economic and Political Weekly, Vol. 11, Issue No. 43–44, 24 October 1959.

Ganatantra Parishad or Democratic Party: Policy Statement, Balangir, Ganatantra Press, 1951.

Ghosh, R., 'The 1948 Blood Bath in Kharsawan', *Mankind*, Vol III. No. 1, Hyderabad, August 1948.

Ministry of Home Affairs, *Report of the States Reorganization Commission*, 1955, https://bit.ly/3L1ojbE. Accessed on 21 March 2022.

Nayak, P.M., 'Sadheikalara Sahityacharcha', *Khabar*, 28 March 2011.

Sahu, N.K. and Nilamani Senapati, *Orissa District Gazetteers: Balangir*, Cuttack Government Press, 1968.

Souvenir 1976, Rajendra Narayan Memorial Committee, Bhubaneswar.

Souvenir 1991, Rajendra Narayan Memoral Committee.

Swatantra Party, *Third National Convention*, Bangalore, 1964.

BOOKS

Abhyankar, G.R., *Problems of Indian States,* Aryabhushan Press, Poona, 1928.

Allen, Charles and Sharada Dwivedy, *Lives of Indian Princes,* Century, 1984.

Azad, A.K., *Indian wins Freedom*, Orient Longman, 1959.

Ashton, S.R., *British Policy towards Indian States, 1905-39*, Curzon Press, London, 1982.

Auber, P., *Rise and Progress of British Power in India*, Vol. I, II and III, Wentworth Press, 2019.

Bailey, F.G., *Politics and Social Change—Orissa in 1959*, University of California Press, 1963.

———, *Caste and the Economic Frontier: A Village in Highland Orissa*, Manchester University Press, 1957.

Banerji, R.D., *History of Orissa*, Vol. 2, Prabasi Press, Calcutta, 1931.

Barton, William, *The Princes of India: With a Chapter on Nepal*, Nisbet, London, 1934.

Bhargava, R.P., *The Chamber of Princes*, Northern Books Centre, New Delhi, 1991.

Butler, Irish, *The Viceroy's Wife: Letters of Alice, Countess of Reading, from India*, Hodder & Stoughton, London, 1969.

Butler, Lord, *The Art of the Possible: The Memoirs of Lord Butler*, Hamish Hamilton, 1971.

Caird, James, *India: The Land and the People (1883)*, Kessinger Publishing, 10 September 2010.

Coupland, Reginald, *India: The Indian Problem*, Oxford University Press, Bombay, 1968.

Churchill, Winston, *My Early Life*, Fontana Books, London, 1965.

Collins, Larry and Dominique Lapierre, *Freedom at Midnight*, Simon and Schuster, 1975.

Cunningham, H.S., *British India and its Rulers*, Kessinger Publishing, 1881.

Deo, P.K., *My Humble Contributions: 1957–1961*, Bhawanipatna,

Orissa, 1961.

Dube, S.C., *India's Changing Villages: Human Factors in Community Development*, Routledge and Kegan Paul, London, 1958.

Dutt, R.C., *The Economic History of India Under Early British Rule*, Routledge, London, 1950.

Erdman, H.L., *Swatantra Party and Indian Conservatism*, Cambridge University Press, 1967.

Fitzroy, Yvoune., *Courts and Camps in India*, Methuen & Co., London, 1926.

Forbes, Rosita., *India of the Princes*, The Right Book Club, London, 1939.

Ghosh, Sunit, *Orissa in Turmoil: A Study in Political Developments,* Sankha Prakashan, 1978.

Gopal, Ram, *British Rule in India: An Assessment*, Asia Publishing House, Bombay, 1963.

Guha, Ramchandra, *India After Gandhi*, Picador India, 2008.

Gunther, John, *Inside Asia*, Hamish Hamilton, 1939.

Gupta, S.C., *Agrarian Relations and Early British Rule in India: A Case Study of Ceded and Conquered Provinces (Uttar Pradesh), 1801–1833*, Asia Publishing House, Bombay, 1963.

Halifax, Lord, *Fullness of Days*, Collins, London, 1957.

Hunter, W.W., et al. *History of Orissa*, N.K. Sahu (eds.), Nalanda, Cuttack, 1981.

Hunter, W.W., *A Brief History of the Indian Peoples*, Morrison and Gibe, Edinburgh, 1881.

Hulton, J.H., *Caste in India: Its Nature, Function, and Origin*, Oxford University Press, Bombay, 1961.

Jeffrey, Robin, *People, Princes & Paramount Power: Society and Politics in the Indian Princely States*, Oxford University Press, Delhi, 1978.

Jhangiani, Motilal A., *Jana Sangh and Swatantra*, Manaktalas, Bombay, 1967.

Lee Warner, William, *The Protected Princes of India*, Macmillan, London, 1986.

Lord, John, *The Maharajas*, Hutchinson & Co., London, 1972.

MacDonald, Ramsay, *The Awakening of India*, Hodder and Stoughton, London, 1911.

Mahatab, H.K., *Beginning of the End*, Students Stores, Cuttack, 1972.

Mandelbaum, David G., *Society in India*, Popular Prakashan, Bombay, 1970.

MacMunn, George, *The Indian States and Princes*, Jarrolds, London, 1936.

Mansfield, Harvey C., *Statesmanship and Party Government: A Study of Burke and Bolingbroke*, University of Chicago Press, 1965.

Menon, V.P., *The Story of the Integration of the Indian States*, Orient Longman, Calcutta, 1956.

Mishra, Somanath, *Rajarshi Rajendra*, Lark Books, Bhubaneswar, 2005.

Mohanty, Surendra, *Patha O Prithvi*, Eastern Media, Bhubaneswar, 1986.

Morris-Jones, W.H., *Government and Politics of India*, Hutchinson, London, 1964.

Mullick, S.C., *Samskshipta Kasala Itihas*, Dalganjan Press, Balangir, 1931.

Morrow, Ann, *Highness: The Maharajahs of India*, Grafton, 1986.

Myrdal, Gunnar, *Beyond the Welfare State*, Gerald Duckworth, London, 1960.

Nicolson, Harold, *King George The Fifth: His Life and Reign*, Constable, London, 1952.

Nehru, Jawaharlal, *An Autobiography*, Bodley Head, London, 1936.

Noorano, A.G., *Ministers' Misconduct*, Vikas Publishing House, New Delhi, 1973.

O'Dwyer, Michael, *India as I knew It, 1885–1925*, Constable and Company, London, 1925.

Ostrogorski, M., *Democracy and the Organization of Political Parties*, Frederick Clarke (trans.), Macmillan, London, 1902.

Palmer, Norman D., *The Indian Political System*, Houghton Mifflin Harcourt, Boston, 1961.

Park, Richard Land and Tinker Irene, *Leadership and Political*

Institutions in India, Oxford University Press, 1960.

Polpai, S.L., *General Elections in India*, Allied Publishers, Bombay, 1962.

Pradhan, P.M., *Muktipath Sainike*, Bhubaneswar, 1973.

Prasad, Rajendra, *An Autobiography*, Asia Publishing House, Bombay, 1957.

Punjabi, K.L., *The Indomitable Sardar*, Bharatiya Vidya Bhavan, Bombay, 1962.

Rajkumar, N.V., *Indian Political Parties*, All India Congress Committee, New Delhi, 1948.

Rath, R.N., *Story of Freedom Movement in Orissa States*, Cuttack, University of Michigan Library, 1964.

Roberts, Andrew, *The Holy Fox: The Life of Lord Halifax* Head of Zeus, 2014.

Samal, J.K., *Princely States of Orissa*, 1905–47, Vohra Publication, Allahabad, 1988.

———, *Orissa under the British Crown, 1858-1905*, S. Chand, New Delhi, 1977.

Sen, D.K., *History of Indian States: Their Rights, Status and Obligations*, Sweet and Maxwell; 1 January 1930.

Sujata, Michaael, *Places of India*, Pavillion Books, 1992.

Suri, Promila and Indira Zaidi, *Impact of British Rule on India Economy*, Raaj Prakashan, New Delhi, 1985.

Trench, C.C., *Viceroy's Agent*, Jonathan Cape, 1987.

Tottenham, E.L., *Highness of Hindustan*, Grayson & Grayson, London, 1934.

Walia, Ramesh, *Prajamandal Movement in East Punjab States*, Punjab University, Patiala, 1972.

Weiner, Myron. *Political Change in South Asia*, Firm KLM, 1963.

———, *India: Politics of Scarcity: Public Pressure and Political Response in India*, Asia Publishing House, Bombay, 1963.

———, *Party Politics in India*, Princeton University Press, 1957.

Index

Aditya Pratap Singh Deo, Raja, 5, 6, 8, 69
adivasis, 69
All-India Garjat Praja Sammilani, 51
Amrit Kaur, Rajkumari, 39
Anup Singh Deo, Raja, 104
Ashoka, 61
Attlee, Clement, 39, 45

Bahadur Kanwar, Raj, 24
Balangir, xi, xiv, 2, 4, 6, 11, 14, 15, 17, 20, 25, 26, 29, 30, 31, 32, 34, 35, 36, 43, 56, 57, 58, 83, 84, 85, 87, 124, 139, 140, 156, 157, 159, 160, 165, 166, 168
Balasore, 64, 83, 140
Ballabh Pant, Govind, 87, 95, 128
Balramgarh Fort, 17
Bharatiya Lok Dal, 156
Bhupinder Singh, Maharajadhiraja, 12, 13
Bihari Bag, 103, 105, 107
BJP, 2
British Crown, 5, 13, 17, 38, 45
British Empire, 16, 38
British India, 3, 13, 24, 42, 45, 46, 48, 62, 68, 117

Cabinet Mission, 44, 45, 47, 78
Central Provinces, 52, 61, 62, 63, 64, 72
Chamber of Princes, 3, 4, 13, 40, 44, 45, 47, 49, 168
Chaturanga, 165, 166
Chauhan dynasty, 5
Chauhans, 60
Chiefs' College, 12, 13
Choudhuri, Nabakrushna, 79, 133
Churchill, Winston, 39
communist, 99, 102
Communist, 56, 99, 131
Communist Party, 87, 100, 128
Congress, 38, 39, 40, 41, 43,

44, 45, 46, 48, 49, 50, 51, 52, 57, 58, 59, 60, 65, 74, 76, 79, 80, 81, 82, 83, 84, 85, 86, 87, 88, 89, 91, 92, 93, 99, 100, 101, 102, 103, 104, 105, 106, 107, 108, 109, 110, 111, 112, 113, 114, 115, 116, 117, 118, 119, 120, 122, 123, 124, 126, 127, 128, 129, 130, 131, 132, 136, 137, 138, 139, 140, 141, 142, 143, 144, 147, 148, 149, 150, 151, 152, 154, 155, 156, 159
Congress (O), 139
Congress (R), 136, 139, 140, 143, 144, 155
Constituent Assembly, 47, 49, 72, 73, 75, 99, 117
Court of Wards, 10, 11, 13, 16

Das, Banka Bihari, 141, 154
Das, Biswanath, 109, 117, 140, 141, 151
Das, Harihar, 101, 103
defection, 141, 144, 145, 149, 150, 154
democracy, xiii, xiv, 41, 55, 58, 59, 77, 84, 85, 87, 88, 99, 120, 144, 145, 148, 171
Deo, Batsraj Singh, 7
Deo, Bhupal Singh, 9, 10
Deo, Brajendra Narayan Singh, 165, 168
Deo, Maharaja Pratap Kesari, 158, 166
Deo, Maharaja Rajendra Narayan Singh, ix, xiii, xv, 2, 4, 14, 167, 172
Dhenkanal, 51, 52, 54, 85, 140, 168
Dilip Kaur of Patiala, Maharani, 13
dominions, 16, 48
Dravidian, 66, 99
Dwivedy, Surendranath, 89

Eastern States Agency, 9, 17, 35, 50, 52, 72
Eastern States Union, 17, 18, 50, 51, 52, 53, 54, 77
Election Commission, 86, 100, 101, 124
Enlai, Zhou, 128

First World War, 13

Ganatantra Parishad, xiv
Gandhi, Indira, xiv, 4, 59, 82, 112, 130, 131, 136, 140, 144, 152
Gandhi, Mahatma, xiv, 34, 38, 39, 44, 46, 51, 54, 58, 86, 112
Garjat Praja Sammilani, 41, 51
Garjats, 5, 27, 28, 33, 37, 43, 44, 50, 52, 53, 56, 62, 69, 77, 86
gauntia, 20, 21
George V, 32
Great Depression, 18

Harijans, xiv, 27
Hindu Mahasabha, 88
Hitler, Adolf, 18, 39

independence, 5, 25, 37, 38, 39, 40, 44, 45, 46, 48, 50, 52, 98, 100, 149, 155, 163
Indian National Congress, 39, 41, 98, 117, 127, 131, 136
Indo-Pakistan War, 129
Industrial Revolution, 16
Instrument of Accession, 55, 69, 70

Janardan Raghunath Mudholkar, Justice, 136
Jharkhand, 4, 13, 65, 66, 82, 124, 139, 140, 143
Jinnah , Mohammed Ali, 44

Kalinga War, 61
Kendu leaf, 134
Keonjhar, 52, 65, 67, 80, 85, 87, 140, 142
Khanna, Justice Hans Raj, 133, 136
Kharsawan, 52, 53, 57, 67, 68, 69, 70, 71, 72, 73, 74, 75, 77, 79, 94, 95, 97
Koshal Utkal Praja Parishad, 59
Kumari, Maharani Kailash, 57, 162, 168
Kumari, Padmini, 5, 6, 7

leader of opposition, 142, 159, 171
legislative Assembly, xiii, 87, 100, 150, 151
Lok Sabha Elections, 85

Mahatab, Harekrushna, 41, 59, 119, 120, 130
Mayo College, 11, 12, 13, 169
Mayurbhanj, 11, 17, 41, 42, 51, 52, 53, 56, 57, 65, 67, 71, 72, 85, 95, 107
Mehta, Balwantrai, 30
Menon, Krishna, 87
Menon, V.P., 3, 53, 54
Mishra, Pt Godabarish, 33, 80, 83
Mitra, Biren, 102, 115, 125, 129
Mohan Mohanty, Braja, 142
Mohan Pradhan, Pabitra, 130, 132, 138
Mohanty, Surendra, 80, 89, 109, 165, 171
Muhammad Hamidullah Khan Bahadur, Nawab, 42
Muslim League, 44, 45, 46, 47, 48

Narayan, Jayaprakash, 89, 112
National Democratic Front, 88, 89
Nehru, Jawaharlal, 30, 101, 112

Odia, 4, 6, 43, 50, 60, 61, 62, 63, 64, 65, 66, 67, 68, 69, 71, 74, 80, 83, 91, 93, 94, 100, 123, 126, 133, 134,

149, 160, 165, 166, 172
Operation Gibraltar, 129
opposition, xiv, 59, 60, 84, 86, 88, 89, 93, 98, 102, 104, 105, 112, 123, 125, 127, 130, 132, 142, 144, 148, 150, 153, 159, 171
Opposition, 76, 86, 88, 91, 99, 102, 103, 104, 105, 110, 111, 124, 128, 142, 145, 150
Orissa Jana Congress, 120, 130, 131, 132, 136, 137, 139, 156
Orissa Pradesh Congress Committee, 76, 79, 123
Orissa State Legislative Assembly, 97
Orissa States Agency, 9, 17

Pant, Govind Ballabh, 87, 95, 128
Patna Dipika, 29, 34, 165
Patnagarh, 17, 30, 31, 32
Patnaik, Biju, 82, 101, 108, 109, 110, 112, 113, 119, 120, 123, 124, 125, 129, 137, 142, 151, 152, 155
Patna State, xiii, 4, 6, 12, 14, 15, 16, 24, 29, 30, 31, 32, 35, 159, 165
Patna State Tenancy Act, 31
post-Independence, 17, 165, 167
Praja Mandal, 40, 51, 54, 75, 84
Praja Socialist Party, 89, 90, 100, 101, 102, 103, 104, 124, 131, 139, 148
Prajatantra, 103, 112
Pratap Chandra Bhanj Deo, Sir, 41
Prithviraj Singh Deo, Maharaja, 4
Public Accounts Committee, 125, 128
Public Service Regulations, 24

Quit India Movement, 38, 39

Radhakrishnan, S., 87
Rajendra Prasad, Dr, 75, 87
Risley, H.H., 62
Routray, Nilamani, 81, 115, 142

Sadar villages, 30
Sailashree Palace, 6, 8, 27, 32, 36, 42, 43, 58, 85
Sailendra Narayan Bhanj Deo, Raja, 111
salute states, 17
Sambalpur, 8, 9, 14, 15, 17, 33, 43, 59, 61, 62, 63, 64, 65, 68, 91, 125, 140
Satpathy, Nandini, 139, 140, 143, 146, 149, 150, 155, 156
Second World War, 3, 18, 34, 35, 39, 98
Senapati, Nilamani, 37
Seraikela, xiii, 4, 5, 6, 7, 8, 9, 11, 12, 52, 57, 67, 68, 69, 70, 71, 72, 73, 74, 75, 77, 79, 81, 82, 93, 94, 95, 97,

100, 165, 168
Sifton, Sir James David, 14
Singhbhum, 63, 65, 66, 68, 70, 74, 79
Singh, Dalganjan, 5, 6
Singh Deo, Batsraj, 7
Sino-Indian War, 128
Socialist Party, 87, 88, 89, 155, 156
Soviet Union, 127, 128
States Reorganisation Commission, 76, 77, 78, 79, 95, 96, 97
Sura Pratap, Maharaja, 5
Swatantra Party, xiv, 60, 93, 126, 127, 131, 132, 136, 138, 139, 140, 141, 142, 144, 149, 150, 151, 152, 153, 155, 156, 170
Tashkent Declaration, 130
The Samaj, 77, 79
Titlagarh, 30, 31, 166
Tripathy, Sadashiva, 130, 132

Uday, Ananga, xv, 159, 173
Utkal Dipika, 165
Utkal Sammilani, 67, 76, 79, 81, 93, 94
Utkal University, 33, 34, 151

Vallabhbhai Patel, Sardar, 3, 53, 112

Wavell, Earl Archibald Percival, 39
Wheeler, Henry, 9

zamindari, 3, 4